THE
LONELY
WARRIORS

The Lonely Warriors

Case for the
Military-Industrial Complex

John Stanley Baumgartner

NASH PUBLISHING
LOS ANGELES

**To Mary
with love**

ALSO BY JOHN STANLEY BAUMGARTNER

Project Management

Handbook of Business Administration
(Contributing Author)

Anatomy of a Merger
(Coauthor)

Foreword

Americans have every reason to feel deep pride in their country's defense establishment and defense industry. The people involved in defense activities have deterred the big war for more than a quarter of a century. They have provided the material for a hot war with minimum disruption to life as usual. They have met every technological and production challenge presented. The industrial complex has even put men on the moon. From the vantage point of not being too close to MIC, the military-industrial complex, French author Jean-Jacques Servan-Schreiber recognizes and gives high praise to the effectiveness of the integrated structure of American Government agencies, corporations, and universities. These same elements are the heart of MIC.

Ironically enough, MIC is under unprecedented attack from the very people who benefit most from it and who could well take pride in its accomplishments. Professors, senators, and writers are among those leading the attack. Some of their criticism is justified; but much is not only unjustified, it is based on preconceived notions, a desire to serve other purposes, or the idea that "it's the popular thing to do." Generally these individuals have demonstrated that they are unencumbered by actual knowledge of defense procurement. Their lop-sided criticisms get headlines, but fall far short of presenting truth.

These attackers are like ax-wielders, chopping away at the poles holding up the big top, the country's protective cover. They attack the capability, integrity, and even the purpose of the military-industrial complex with great gusto. All American taxpayers, in or out of defense-related activities, are interested in getting the most for our defense dollar. But we may find one day that those chopping at the tent poles have finally brought down the tent, to their own surprise.

Much has been said about the bigness of MIC, as if this alone makes it suspect. The fact is that less than one-sixth of the total business of the twenty-five largest defense contractors is defense oriented; five-sixths is not related to defense. It is clear that these companies can do without defense business, restrictions, and criticism more easily than can the country do without their services. As abuse and unwarranted criticism accumulate, however, these companies may well turn away from defense and let less-qualified firms carry the defense burden.

People who have been in both the military establishment and the defense industry recognize the integrity, devotion, selflessness, and tremendous collective abilities of people in MIC—the Lonely Warriors who provide the protective cover for us and for much of the free world. Theirs is a lonely war, just as this is a lonely book compared to the stacks of volumes and articles that would tear away this protective cover.

This book is intended to show why much of the criticism levelled at MIC is fallacious, and to show the procurement game as it really is. It's about the biggest undiscovered show on earth.

Stan Baumgartner
Northridge, California
January, 1970

Contents

THE
LONELY
WARRIORS

1
The Siege of the Military-Industrial Complex

Depending on how you look at it, this is the Space Age, Nuclear Age, Free-Loader Age, Old Age, Dangerous Age, Permissive Age, Jet Age, Teen Age, Civil Rights Age, or Hippie Age. It is a Threshold Age, with dimensions only dimly perceived. It's an Age for All Purposes and an Age for the Multi-Purpose Expert.

It's also a Frustrating Age, due to high prices, Vietnam, domestic troubles, and high taxes. It's a time that calls for finding a target to blame for these frustrations, and loud voices are shouting exuberantly, "We've found it! It's this military-industrial complex!"

The intended target and innocent bystanders (if any *are* innocent) are blasted with rare gusto, and smoke from the fusillade engulfs anyone old enough to read. One senator aims a blunderbuss at the "military-industrial-labor-university complex," picking up in his sights the military and militant SDS-ers at universities. A congressman puckishly adds politicians, thereby enlarging the complex to "military-industrial-political-labor-university complex" or MIPLUC. Another senator says, "Maybe we should call it an 'economic-educational-scientific-military-industrial complex,' which becomes LEEPSMIC. A trigger-happy blast from the *Atlanta Constitution* grazed North American Rockwell for problems on the F-111B fighter-bomber—produced by General Dynamics.

The attack on MIC (military-industrial complex)/MIPLUC (military-industrial-political-labor-university complex)/LEEPSMIC (economic-educational-scientific-military-industrial complex) gets serious, however, when it strikes at the winner of the West and victor of Iwo Jima, Saipan, Philippines, and the European Theater: all-time hero John Wayne. A New York Congressman, intent on ambushing the head of Batjac Productions, unloosed a barrage at the Army and at the producer of "The Green Berets." Fortunately in the exchange of shots, everyone's hero came through unscathed, still ready for all comers.

It's hard to tell the good guys from the bad guys though, particularly when the good guys say they're good, and the bad guys and some good guys call them bad. It's as if they mixed up all the white and black hats and then drew them by lot. In the resulting mix-up some of the hats are the wrong color, and some don't fit ("Who turned out the lights?").

One reason for the confusion surrounding the frustration surrounding MIC is that we find experts zooming far outside their fields of expertise to get in a few words on the so-called military-industrial complex. In their combined wisdom and ignorance, scientists, baby doctors, professors, and others have become, by osmosis or lateral transfer, experts on MIC. They're in the wrong game, on the wrong set; but they're there, and it makes the natives a little restless. Let's look at a few cameo roles. Ready?

In this one we see a kindly doctor giving advice on babies to young mothers. Then, in the next take, apparently a flash-back or a flash-forward, the same doctor, face distorted, is leading a group of angry militants, shouting, waving fists, threatening someone off-screen.

On another set, a picture about a crusading economics professor in an Ivy League school, we see a brief sequence in which he yells, "All right, everyone back in the arsenal!" as he points to an ancient structure in the background.

In another picture, a young politician in a big city is on the phone. At the other end, in a jungle area, is a troop commander engaged in directing a military operation, ricochets whining in the background. The politician is saying, "Now you shouldn't be doing it that way! You're over there to—say, how come you're over there anyway?"

"I'm sorry Senator—I was just about to lead an attack up a hill. Can we talk about it another time?" (A mortar round explodes nearby, cutting the phone connection.) The Senator looks at his phone, disgruntled, and jams it back on its cradle.

In this one, a picture about submarines, an individual in naval uniform is giving close-order drill to a group of civilians who, it turns out, are corporate controllers. "Dress right . . . Dress! (moves to right flank of platoon) Bring it up a little, GD . . . back, Lockheed; up a little LTV and GE . . . up on the end. Hold it! Ready . . . Front! (takes position in front of platoon) Now today I want you men to prepare for inspection, and I want you to have your statements *uniform*. You got that? Accounting months exactly the same length; costs by item, rather than organiza-

tion; and I want your duffel bags to include the following overhead items. . . ."

In addition to experts out of orbit, a major reason for
confusion is newsworthiness, What Will Make News Today.
The facts often are clearer before interpreters of the news
insert themselves between the action and the reader. The
Dave 'n Drew incident is an example.

> One morning columnist Drew Pearson, with informa-
> tion straight from the inside, recounted how one
> Capt. Dave Miller, Contracting Officer in The Army
> Signal Supply Agency in Philadelphia, had awarded
> a contract to a company at a price well over twice
> what the same equipment had previously cost. It was
> an item purchased for the Navy, and in excess costs
> (apparently excess profits At Your Expense, Tax-
> payer), the award was some $200,000 more than
> had previously been paid for the same identical item.
> Drew's informer hadn't bothered with all the
> facts; or for some reason they didn't get into the col-
> umn. Sure the cost was more than twice previously
> paid—because the item had been out of production
> for some time and it would cost that much to set up
> for it again. Dave had queried the Navy, In view of
> the higher cost, do you still want the item? The Navy
> said Sure, Dave, it's needed as part of a major com-
> munications system.
> Dave got the contractor's price; it was more
> than twice the amount previously paid. Do you still
> want it, Navy? Same answer. Dave made the award,
> and the contractor produced at a nominal profit,
> although it caused considerable dislocation of his
> normal production work. The whole story, including
> the rationale for an award, isn't nearly as newsworthy
> as half the story, however.

How can the reader of national affairs expect to know "what's behind some of these goofy awards" when he's given only part of the picture? Who can blame him for wondering, "How can these guys be so stupid?"

Here's another one. Headline: GM Awarded Contract for Millions More Than Small Company's Bid. The Story: Army wastes millions on procurement of M-16 rifle, when a company in Saco, Maine bid $20 million under giant General Motors. There, isn't that favoring big business? Doesn't that prove waste, favoritism, sleeping with, stupidity, favoritism, culpability, inefficiency, favoritism? We've got you this time, MIC!

Only, someone who remembered World War II's broomstick brigade must have asked, "Can the outfit in Maine produce?" There isn't much that's more basic to defense than a rifle, from Revolutionary days to now (sometimes the two periods seem to coincide), and the questioner must have had strong doubts that the outfit in Maine could deliver M-16's on time. What happens if a patrol gets shot at; should it point broomsticks and yell, "Bang, you're dead"? Can the Contracting Officer soothe the broomstickers' mothers with, "Sure the low bidder isn't producing—but he assured us he would, and besides we saved $20 million on the deal. Your sons' buddies will be getting M-16's any week now." Decision: go with assured delivery.

Most of the spine-tinglers in the procurement game pertain to R&D—research and development, inventing things that turn out costing several times the original estimate. One day the headlines pinpointed DSRV, the deep submersible rescue vehicle being built for the Navy: the contractor's costs had ballooned to a record twenty-seven times the original estimate! What wasn't reported is that the original estimate was a guesstimate and that the DSRV being developed bears little resemblance to the original DSRV because of directed changes in purpose and design. The contractor, in fact, is doing a very commendable job.

Here's another spine-tingler. Costs of developing a 1300 m.p.h. aircraft have risen from an estimate of $360 million to $1.6 *billion*, with only 30 percent of the technical problems solved after seven years' effort, and well below performance on one critical specification! Doesn't *that* make your tax-paying blood boil? And even on a relatively simple ship modification— new air conditioning units, electrical systems, hot and cold water systems, etc., with *no* R&D involved—the cost of one project is at least *five times* the original estimate and the project itself more than a year behind schedule! (The seething, how-ever, must be reserved for outsiders. The plane in question is the British-French Concorde and the ship, the Queen Mary.)

Optimism emerges as one of the culprits in the unfold-ing half-told stories of the C-5A aircraft, main battle tank, Navy shipbuilding and other procurements. "You contractors should submit higher—more realistic—proposals on these breakthrough projects!" Sure there's optimism, and the overruns that often result cause anguish all around, particularly in Congress; but can it truly be said the taxpayer isn't getting his money's worth? And can any businessman, in any industry, stay in business if he's *pessimistic* about how well or how soon or for how much he can do a job? So, over the years, the Dave 'n Drew incidents, the M-16 and C-5A incidents, and the procurement procedure itself are reported as the fat-cat life of the MIC/ MIPLUC/LEEPSMIC. The reader has a tough time fathoming the truth about procurement when he gets only bits of the truth and is served with conclusions based on these bits.

There's a third fundamental reason for the confusion surrounding MIC, in addition to out-of-orbit experts and deceptive reporting. Lending its voice to the raucous noise about MIC is a group that couldn't care less about national priorities or procurement efficiency. Its objective is to cause the nation to take off its armor or let the shield and sword disintegrate with rust. This group's voice sounds much like those of the experts and the partial-reporters; the difficulty is in distinguishing intent. But can anyone seriously believe that *none* of the confusion surrounding the shoot-out springs from the pink fringe? (Witches might cackle, "Shades of Salem, 1680!" Witches decry witch hunts.)

But this book isn't about witches or witch hunters or witch doctors. And it's not about Here's How the C-5A Overrun Is Justified, or Why We Should Have An ABM. It's about who makes the decisions and how, where the money goes and who tries to control it, and how companies get those Fat Government Contracts. It's about the heart of the military-industrial interface, where the exchange of dollars takes place. The purpose of this book is to give you a ringside seat—and let you dangle a foot in the tigers' arena—in the biggest undiscovered show on earth.

A great American once said:

> Now this conjunction of an immense military establishment and a large arms industry is new in the American experience. The total influence—economic, political, even spiritual—is felt in every city, every state house, every office of the Federal Government. In the councils of Government, we must guard against the acquisition of unwarranted influence, whether sought or unsought, by the military-industrial complex. The potential for the disastrous rise of misplaced power exists and will persist.

This, of course, was President Eisenhower in his oft-quoted farewell address of January 17, 1961.

But in a part of the speech that is rarely noted, and never quoted by critics of MIC, he also said:

> Until the latest of our world conflicts, the United States had no armaments industry. American makers of plowshares could, with time and as required, make swords as well.
>
> *But we can no longer risk emergency improvisation of national defense.* (Italics added) We have been compelled to create a permanent armaments industry of vast proportions. . . .

The lag-time that allowed two years' preparation ('39-'41) for an all-out hassle thirty years ago has been reduced to a matter of minutes at the present time. Emergency improvisation in the '70s is getting in the ring with Joe Frazier and saying at the last second, "Hold it, Joe; I'd like a few more months for training and road work." The awkward part is that Joe just might not go along with the request.

MIC is big; it reportedly employs one in every ten working Americans if one includes draftees, DOD (Department of Defense) civilians, regular military, people in cities near military installations, and all the workers in the thousands of defense-supplying companies (which also produce commercial and industrial products). (Defense sales of the twenty-five largest contractors actually accounted for less than *one-sixth* of their total sales in 1968.) But Eisenhower probably had in mind only the core of this diverse gang, the industrial, technical, and military personnel directly involved in producing goods for the military. Ninety-five percent of the military, for instance, have never been involved in procurement. The portion of MIC that is actively involved, full or part time, in providing goods for the military is probably less than a million people.

The annual procurement dollar is no small potatoes either: about $20 billion is earmarked for annual procurement, plus an additional $7.5 billion or so for RDTE—research, development, test and evaluation, largely performed by industrial contractors. (Procurement and RDTE together account for more than one-third of the DOD budget.) If this were in ten-dollar bills laid end to end, the Apollo astronauts could scoop them up all the way to the moon.

It's big.

Still, the proportion of gross national product that goes for defense has actually gone *down*, from about 10 percent in 1967 to 8 percent at the present time. (Secretary of Defense Laird has noted that the nation's unpreparedness in 1939, when only 1 percent of the GNP was spent for defense, put the country in no position to stop Hitler and limited U.S. fighting effectiveness for a full year after Pearl Harbor. He notes also, "All the financial 'savings' of a decade evaporated in one month's wartime spending.") And if a lot of people are involved in producing the hardware and software required for defense, they are nevertheless only one-half of one percent of the population. These people, in both industry and the military, are probably more dedicated and are certainly more steadfast than their counterparts in active wartime; and in spite of having prevented the big war for twenty-five years, their contribution to the rest of their countrymen goes not only unappreciated but the defenders are themselves attacked. Theirs is the loneliest war.

Well, why did the late former President, a national hero, discuss the Military-Industrial Complex at all? Wasn't he a career part of it? Yes and no. During more than a half century of service, from cadet to Commander-in-Chief, he was involved in the *use* of the military means, rather than in *procurement* of the means; he was one of the 95 percent not directly concerned with procurement. And he was in a key position to observe the military's increasing reliance on industry and scientific organizations for bringing weapon and support systems into being. The change in hardware in the mid-fifties was from massive quantities of relatively simple items, as produced in World War II, to much fewer but more highly sophisticated items. This formed part of the background for his comments on MIC.

The President also had observed the skirmish between the backers of the Bomarc missile and the backers of the Nike Hercules; and he was stung by the fact that the skirmish spilled over into advertising and attempts to influence opinion. It might be remembered, however, that this was a period when the Services' roles and missions were less clearly defined— particularly as to short-range missiles, close-support aircraft, and strategic systems—because of new capabilities.

The outgoing President also noted that the evolution of sophisticated systems placed great demands on technical and scientific know-how. These changes required the best management and technical talent, wherever it could be found. Clearly this was something new, compared to the limited capabilities of Government-operated arsenals and laboratories.

Since that time, the critics of MIC have quoted the farewell address in and out of context, and have added a wide variety of charges in what amounts to an informal court martial, with the general public sitting on the court, and some of the court growling, "Bring the guilty bastard in!"

The broadside includes a wide variety of charges, with practically everything but the printing press being hurled at it. Interestingly, no one accuses MIC of failing to do its job; but this seems to be overlooked.

By way of setting the stage for how MIC works—the inner core of MIC—it's worthwhile to summarize these various charges:

- ☐ Excess profits.

- ☐ Arms costs purposely understated; "chronic over-optimism." Contractors and DOD play games with each other.

- ☐ Muzzled testimony.

- ☐ Huge amounts of waste; great overruns on current programs, and billions spent on programs subsequently cancelled.

- ☐ Poor management by the Pentagon; it "can cut the defense budget by at least $10 billion without reducing our effectiveness."

- ☐ Failure by heads of five major defense companies to appear before a Senate committee.

- ☐ Inflated military budgets that create inflation throughout the economy.

- ☐ Unholy alliance of military, industry, labor, universities, etc.

- ☐ Skimming off the cream of scientific talent.

- ☐ 2,072 former military procurement officers now on contractors' payrolls.

- ☐ A former Assistant Secretary of Defense now with a leading contractor (where 1 percent of his group's business is defense).

The charges come from a vociferous former Marine
Corps commandant, various members of Congress, professors,
pediatricians, economists, and others on the inside and outside.
The scramble in the dark for white hats, and for clamping the
black hats on others, is a wondrous thing to behold.

MIC is not without its defenders, including representatives and senators who have a responsibility for preparedness,
industrial leaders, some DOD officials, a small proportion of
average taxpayers who have no direct contact with MIC, and
far-sighted observations by Generals of the Army MacArthur
and Marshall. But its defenders have a difficult task.

The *Manual for Courts Martial* says, "It is true that
rape is a most detestable crime . . . but it must be remembered
that it is an accusation easy to be made, hard to be proved,
but harder to be defended by the party accused, though
innocent."

As MIC's critics snowball, it might be well to recall,
again, these words by Theodore Roosevelt:

> It is not the critic who counts; not the man who points
> out how the strong man stumbled or where the doer
> of deeds could have done them better.
>
> The credit belongs to the man who is actually
> in the arena; whose face is marred by dust and sweat
> and blood; who strives valiantly; who errs and comes
> short again and again; who knows the great enthusi-
> asms, the devotions, and spends himself in a worthy
> cause.
>
> Who, at the best, knows the triumph of high
> achievement; and who, at the worst, if he fails, at
> least fails while daring greatly, so that his place shall
> never be with those cold and timid souls who knew
> neither victory nor defeat.

2
MIC,
Seen Darkly

Blasting away at MIC has long been a sort of national pastime, rivaling baseball and more popular participant sports. One of the satisfactions is that the blasters know the target is out there somewhere, and it's so big they're bound to hit something, whatever their aim.

It's hard to know whether to laugh or cry at some of the myths and folklore generated by these blasts. Mostly, the badmouthing wouldn't be credible enough to comment on because MIC's defense, if it needs one, is its record: it performs. But the problem is that when the badmouthing is repeated often and loud enough it becomes believable, and some of the appointed members of MIC seem themselves to be among the blasters. En route to more enlightening aspects of MIC, therefore, it's probably worth looking at the nature of some of these unkind cuts.

At the crying end of the scale is the lack of backing and even misinformation provided by high DOD officials, who occasionally serve as ammo bearers for the blasters. The reported all-time record overrun, 2,600 percent or so, is an example.

At the hilarious end is a critic who hasn't yet experienced his first day in uniform who writes, "In the fifties it required courage for a civilian to challenge Eisenhower on military matters. Anyone is allowed to doubt the omniscience of General Westmoreland." This reflects the "Twinkle, Twinkle Little Star" school, for whom this ditty wraps up about all there is on astronomy, space exploration, and general officers.

Between these purveyors of tears and guffaws are the informers who interpret and repeat The Word so that all of us poor clods in the general public will *understand—"really understand"*—what's going on. The problem in "really understanding" is that the interpreters themselves are often so painfully under-informed. These include not only the analysts and observers of the news who are clueing us in on the show they have discovered, but also legislators dabbling for the first time in defense procurement.

Here's how the information game works.

BIRTH OF A MYTH. OR IS IT A FACT?

"...the subcommittee chairman, Sen. William Proxmire (D-Wis.) came up with what appears to be the current record for cost growth," a news release announces. "He charged that the price of the Navy's deep submersible rescue vehicle (DSRV) has jumped from $3 million each in 1964 to $80 million currently, an increase of almost 2,700 percent." The DSRV program was born following the unfortunate *Thresher* disaster in 1963, for the purpose of rescuing sailors trapped in a disabled submarine.

On June 11, 1969, Senator Proxmire asked the Assistant Secretary of Defense (Installations and Logistics) to con-
firm that the DSRV Program had increased in cost from $36.5
million for twelve vehicles to $480 million for six vehicles, or
from $3 million to $80 million per vehicle. The Assistant
Secretary answered affirmatively. And incorrectly. The whop-
ping cost increase was duly repeated and embellished numerous
times as a horrible example of waste, inefficiency, laxity, and
so on. MIC's critics had a field day.

The belated truth is that the program was never priced
at $36.5 million. This oft-repeated figure was someone's
unofficial guesstimate, without significant design study by either
the Navy or by industry, and failed to include, among other
things, development costs. There was never a contract at this
figure. The Navy's first official cost estimate was $120 million,
for a six-vehicle program. The higher subsequent estimate was
for a rescue vehicle of markedly greater capability (greater
mating capability with the distressed submarine, air transporta-
bility, and capacity for twenty-seven rather than twenty per-
sons) and included Navy costs for operation, support and
maintenance for ten years.

The myth, however, is stronger than the truth, particularly when it comes from an apparently knowledgeable source.

ASSUMPTIONS THAT BECOME FACTS

One observer writes, "Former Assistant Secretary of
Defense Robert Charles could not recall for Proxmire when
he'd last seen a major defense contractor lose money on a contract." This is then reported as *fact*: major defense contractors
haven't lost money on contracts in a coon's age. As almost
everyone was aware by the time the observer's article was writ-

ten, Lockheed lost quite a chunk on the C-5A, and a little research would reveal a number of other money-losing defense contracts in other companies. To many readers, however, this observer's assumption became fact.

MISINTERPRETATION

In the same publication, portraying defense and industry figures in cartoons and caricatures, the editors remarkably hoped to "shed light and stir action where both have been lacking too long." Its Washington editor then proceeded to blot out some of the already dim light with examples such as this: ". . . when a manager of a weapons-system procurement finds that costs are outrunning the money Congress gave him, he has a 'funding problem.' In other words, costs are not too high, his funds are too low . . . what (Proxmire's witnesses) are telling us is that bargain and cost control, 'twixt military and contractor, is not gimlet-eyed jockeying in the best sense of free enterprise. It is more the murmuring of lovers."[1]

The limited background of the under-informed informer comes through in concluding "in other words, costs are not too high, his funds are too low." It doesn't translate that way. Here's why:

On a $100 million program scheduled over a thirty-month period, the contractor and his subcontractors are performing very well. In fact, they are two months ahead of schedule, as the program goes into its final twelve months. But there's a problem: at the eighteen-month point they've spent $70 million whereas the funding plan called for spending only $60 million. For the actual progress they've made, however (twenty months' progress), it was expected that they would have spent

$72 million. In other words, they're *below* the estimated cost for the progress achieved. Nevertheless, they have a *funding* problem, because the additional $10 million required hasn't yet been allocated.

In other words, costs in this case truly are not too high; funds are too low.

In the best-managed of programs, as well as overrun programs, funding problems are exactly that; "funding problem"is not a play on words, as the magazine writer clearly interpreted the term to mean. In real life his "murmuring of lovers" is more like a wounded grizzly charging a hunter and the hunter fighting for his life. As noted in Chapters 8 and 10, the conflict is fierce and takes its toll.

SELECTIVE TUNING

With so many individuals expressing opinions on the MIC, it's easy to pick a backer for any point of view. Eisenhower's farewell can support either the defender or attacker of MIC, for instance. (The fact is that the speech, prepared by Dr. Malcolm Moos, is vague.) One can easily tune it to whatever argument serves his purpose. In the same way, critics will overlook successes such as Polaris, Apollo and the A-7 aircraft in selective criticism of other programs produced by the same companies.

In one of the longer stretches to make a point, Washington's largest morning newspaper headlines as an "official report" the conclusions of a minor Bureau of the Budget bureaucrat on waste in the Pentagon, written for his Princeton University master's thesis. A senator praises colleagues who share his views on MIC, while terming those with opposing views "stooges of the military."

WEASEL WORDS

Related to selective tuning is the matter of weasel words —words that are hardly noticed but which serve as an escape hatch if a statement is later torpedoed. Here's an example:

> Practically freed of the fiscal limitations that restrain other agencies, the Pentagon seems to be able to exercise its will in almost any area it chooses, foreign or domestic, from negotiating a new lease for bases and promising military assistance to Spain (as it was recently alleged to have done) to launching programs of social reform.[2]

Hardly noticeable in this sentence is the word "alleged." The facts in the matter are that an Air Force major general carried out the negotiations with Spain, because Congress charged the Defense Department with this responsibility, and DOD in turn assigned the task to the Air Force. "Alleged" enables the spokesman to deliver his punch while providing a defense if someone throws a counterpunch.

OVERRUNS

Overruns have been, are, and undoubtedly will be a continuing problem. But the record is getting better. Prior to former Defense Secretary McNamara's changing the ground rules on development contracts from cost-plus-fixed-fee contracts to incentive contracts, overruns often amounted to several times the original contract estimate. McNamara, however, shifted the greater part of risks for overruns from the Government to industry, and overruns were greatly reduced, both in number of cases and in dollar volume. This occurred not so much because final prices were different, but because proposal prices were more realistic, i.e., higher. At the same time, however, contractors' profits have been hurt (Chapter 5) to the extent that the most capable contractors have less and less incentive to stay in the defense business.

In Defense Secretary Laird's initial report on twelve programs to the Senate's Armed Services Committee, optimistic original cost estimates accounted for 40 percent of the cost growth reported. Laird has subsequently said, in effect, "You contractors have got to come in with higher cost estimates!"

There's no question that overruns are a frustrating problem—to the Defense Department and to a Congress that believes it has already provided sufficient funds for a program.

But there are differing reasons for overruns. A statement on overruns reads:

> . . . it must be recognized that *loss of project control,* whether due to negligence, ineptness *or other reason* is a burden the country cannot afford. Dollars wasted *through loss of control* are dollars which, in a critical fiscal period, could prevent the deadlining of tanks in Korea and the grounding of SAC bombers. They are the dollars that could improve the payload of a space vehicle or the reliability of a booster. . . . It is understandable that where pushing the calendar and pushing the state of the art require cost-type contracts, there will be overruns and schedule slippages. Advancing into the unknown is bound to be preceded by inaccurate estimates. *Overruns and slippages because of loss of control are considerably different from the same effects caused by imperfect foresight, however.*[3]

The C-5A, which has glittered in the limelight as a prime example of overruns, starred in this role for the wrong reason. The program has been well managed by a highly professional team, and the performance of the huge cargo aircraft has been outstanding, as even critics will admit. The C-5A overruns were not, as critics imply, due to ulterior motives or lackadaisical management. The basic problem was imperfect foresight: costs of labor, materials, equipment, and subcontracts that rocketed far faster than previous experience indicated they would, and admittedly optimistic beliefs minimizing the problems posed by the sheer size and technology of the plane.

The package procurement concept also was roundly criticized in its first application on the C-5A. Nevertheless it has the saving grace of resulting in a considerably lower cost to the Government than if successive contracts, from development through operational support, had been negotiated.

Prior to this contract, a common complaint was that the winner of development-phase competition was "locked in" for the succeeding production contract, and he could therefore set and hold firm to a higher price. Package procurement precluded this by providing one contractor for the whole program package, at a very competitive total price. The concept and its originator, former Air Force Assistant Secretary Robert H. Charles, have been castigated, however, by people having no knowledge of contracting.

One relatively sure way to avoid future criticism, in contracting as in hardware, is to avoid progress.

"I THINK IT WOULD BE NICE IF WE SPENT . . ."

A Gallup Poll asked interviewees whether they thought defense spending was too much, too little, or about right.[4] Surprisingly, only 52 percent thought "too much"; 31 percent said "about right," 8 percent, "too little," and 9 percent, no opinion. The poll then asked whether the interviewees "happened to recall" how much is spent for defense. Seventy-one percent were unable to answer the question.

"As the survey reported indicates," the poll concluded, "the typical citizen is by no means knowledgeable about the details of the U.S. defense program. His judgment is formed mainly on the basis of impressions he gets from public discussion and from the debate in Washington between the Pentagon and certain groups in Congress."

Popular magazines, however, rush in to present what the defense budget should be, presumptuous as this may seem. One publication says the 1972 budget (assuming Vietnam costs could largely be eliminated by then) should be 22 percent less than DOD is likely to request, and even 10 percent below 1965's budget; this, in spite of the fact that inflation (25 percent in five years) means that a dollar buys less defense than it did in 1965. The article then details where these cuts should be made (e.g., an $11 billion cut in tactical forces).

Another budget version goes along with what just about anyone proposes as a reduction, whatever the basis, including a change in tactical units' tables of organization and equipment (T/O&E), T/O&E's reflect combat and support needs as determined from vast combat experience; but this estimate figures on saving more than $4 billion by merely shuffling some support troops. Advice on spending comes easily when the advisor has meager experience and he doesn't bear the burden of responsibility.

Another observer comments, "Today's military leaders have come to senior rank expecting a level of financial support that would have been the envy of generations of predecessors." He overlooks General of the Army George C. Marshall, among others, who said, "We finish each bloody war with a feeling of acute revulsion against the savage form of human behavior. And yet on each occasion we confuse military preparedness with the causes of war and then drift almost deliberately into another catastrophe."

THE PROBLEM WITH ABSOLUTES

A Harvard biologist and Nobel prize winner, Professor George Wald, says, "Just before World War II the entire American Army, including the Air Force, numbered 139,000 men. Now there are 3.5 million (in all Services) under arms. A total of one million men is surely enough."

A million men could be 111,000 baseball teams, or 200,000 basketball teams.

Absolutes often miss the point, however: big or small *compared to what?* When one of the other teams also has 3.5 million men under arms, one million *invites* aggression, just as the too-small 1939 Army did.

In the same way that absolutes in people can be misleading, absolutes in the costs of defense programs that are cancelled or suspended before completion look enormous. MIC has some explaining to do about "those stupid mistakes on cancelled programs," as we shall see in the next chapter.

THE CONTRARINESS OF MIC

MIC has a talent for ignoring the whims of its various critics. The chief executives of five of the largest defense contractors—Boeing, North American Rockwell, Lockheed, General Dynamics and Litton Industries—declined an invitation to testify on the military budget and national priorities before the Proxmire committee because these matters are outside their scope. Senator Proxmire then called them "new isolationists" and accused them of being "sanctimonious and uncooperative." He further stated that it was their "patriotic duty" to appear.

In an historical parallel to this contrary attitude, the man on the scaffold said to Marie Antoinette, "We'd like to have your viewpoint on this operation, Marie. Now don't be uncooperative—just put your head here on this block. It's your patriotic duty to let us know what you think about this instrument."

The Department of Defense, too, has failed to please all taxpayers. A columnist commends the Defense Secretary for lopping $3 billion off the 1970 budget, but then complains that the Services have clung to the weapons and strategic doctrines *that most offend the critics!*[5] The Navy, for instance, clings to its concept of a war at sea; the Air Force reduces flight training hours rather than its concept of coordinated air strikes; and the Army stands by its "cushy military installations in Western Europe." "The critics enjoyed considerable success in holding down total defense spending," he says. "But their assaults have only hardened support for particular weapons and strategic doctrines." He then proposes that greater pressure on defense spending might cause MIC to get the message about continuing to offend its critics.

Another observer recounts the growing strategic nuclear power of the Russians and the Red Chinese efforts to develop a nuclear striking force; the Soviet Union's growing submarine and surface fleets; and new fighter aircraft. Then he says, "Military men tend to want to meet enemy forces on a one-to-one basis regardless of great differences between the U.S. and its potential enemies. . . ." Military men are funny that way.

Congressional pressure on overseas capabilities may also arouse MIC's balky nature. Some congressmen want to close a substantial number of overseas bases (which seems reasonable); *and* curtail the fleet of C-5A transports which would provide overseas airlift for U.S. troops; *and* reduce the number of floating airbases, the Navy's aircraft carriers. DOD will probably point out that America has global responsibilities and cannot afford to do away with *all three* of these means.

DOD's next fitness report is likely to show low ratings on "cooperation" and "tact."

ABOUT THOSE RETIREES . . .

On the assumption where there's smoke there's fire, the Proxmire committee dug into whatever became of those retired senior officers now in the defense industry. It failed to uncover the fact that the Defense Department has authority to cancel a retired officer's pension if he takes a sales job with a firm that sells to DOD, and failed to uncover similar corporate restrictions against using retired military officers in selling activities. As a matter of fact it failed to uncover evidence of either wrongdoing or rightdoing. But it did smoke out two colonels (M.D.'s) who are now doctors on the staff of Chrysler and General Motors; and the fact surfaced that two other former colonels are now employed in Howard Hughes' Las Vegas casinos. The survey also found that the largest firms employ more of these retired officers than do smaller firms. An attempt was made to relate the matter of retirees to development of the anti-ballistic missile system (ABM); but the attempt went awry when it was discovered that only nine of them are with AT&T, whose Western Electric Company is prime contractor for ABM. AT&T, sixth among 1968's largest prime contractors, ranks only fortieth in its recruitment of senior retirees.

CONCLUSION

As these shots ricochet off Fortress MIC, even MIC's supporters acknowledge that there are weak spots, that there

is room for greater efficiency and less waste. But this is like
experts in the military art bowing to color-blind art critics. In
most cases the facts justify a strong defense or engaging the
attacker on his own ground.

Meanwhile some of MIC's critics have suggestions of
their own, such as:

☐ Spending several hundred million dollars on data
that might be useful in reducing the cost of defense programs.

☐ Nationalizing all defense firms that do more than
75 percent of their business with the Government, a return to the arsenal concept.

☐ Establishing a Military Audit Commission, made
up of scientists and citizens (and excluding "the
military power") that would be an authoritative
voice on weapons systems.

Anyone who can come up with rib-ticklers like these
substitutes for reason can't be all bad.

Let's look now at an area that even MIC's supporters
shy away from, waste due to cancelled programs.

3
It's Stupid To Make Mistakes

For all the wealth and talent it has commanded, however, the military-industrial complex has, through the years, made some big mistakes. (So says an article in the *Chicago Daily News.*)

The Pentagon recently compiled a list of sixty-eight major weapons systems that cost nearly $10 billion—slightly more than all the money the Government proposes to spend for education in the year beginning July.

. . . the $10 billion list was a catalog of abandoned projects that included mistakes and misjudgments on weapons systems fit only for museums or the scrap heap.[1]

The sixty-eight systems included the Air Force B-70 manned bomber, Air Force missiles such as Navaho, Skybolt and Mobile Minuteman; Navy missiles Sparrow I and II, Triton, Oriole and Typhon; and Army missiles Hermes, Terrier and Mauler.

"The list was also a forceful reminder that the military-industrial complex is hardly infallible," the article continues.

How damning can an indictment be?

Here's an insight into what the taxpayer/consumer pays for as revealed by insiders, the executives responsible for costly development programs:

> We find that development-cost overruns, while not serious in themselves, are often symptoms of difficulties encountered in meeting design objectives and that these troubles often lead to higher manufacturing costs . . . adverse variance in engineering costs is something to be avoided if at all possible, but its effect on a product program, as I have said, is fairly insignificant.

> The (development) effort, in short, is on-going, all-inclusive, and basic to company survival. Not only are there enormous possibilities for waste, but the job is never done. . . . Companies have learned the hard way that old favorites can lose their appeal overnight . . . and, as a result, how vulnerable they are.

> *What has been irretrievably spent or committed to date is of concern only in judging the credibility of our forecasts from this point forward.* (Italics added.) The fact that we may already have invested heavily should not make us continue a project which doesn't promise an adequate return on the additional dollars of investment required, nor should it cause us to stop a project which we feel certain will make a good return on the additional investment but will not adequately recoup what we have put in it to date. In the latter situation, we were obviously foolish to have started the program, but we would be equally foolish to stop it at this point.

These detached, almost clinical revelations of development costs continue with these admissions:

It is usually true that the smaller the company, the less it will cost to manufacture a given product, assuming that the company has or can afford the required facilities. Thus a product that can be manufactured by companies appreciably smaller than ours will quite likely be cheaper for them to make. . . . The bigger the requirements for a given product the safer it is, in our view, from lower-cost competition.

How much is spent (on research) must depend on whatever complex balance of income and outgo results in a satisfactory return on invested resources. The extent to which *basic* as opposed to *applied* research is to be encouraged again is a matter for management decision. . . . Perhaps only the largest firms can afford the luxury of much basic research; the majority, of all sizes . . . restrict most R&D to projects which can be expected to pay off, in the predictable future. . . .

Standing still in a company is a frightening thing! One danger that is seldom mentioned is the human tendency in a static organization to tolerate mediocrity. . . . Also, there is the need to keep volume growing at least as fast as overhead. Besides all of Parkinson's laws, many internal and external forces tend to raise indirect expense. This is another seldom acknowledged reason for aiming at continual expansion. . . .

Here we have an almost classic review of the capitalist business panorama: the fascination with profit, cutting off new projects in midstream where additional profits are endangered, recognition of mediocrity in organizations, lack of concern for millions of dollars already spent ("of concern only in judging the credibility of our forecasts from this point forward"), big business looking for ways to gain an advantage, lack of concern about development-cost overruns!

There's an O. Henry twist here, however.

The philosophy expressed in these quotations, and it's eminently sound, pertains to development of *new commercial and industrial products*—hula hoops, Biz soaps, color TV sets, and Mavericks. The quotes are from the American Management Association's book, *New Products/New Profits*[2] and reflect business leaders' recognition of the *premium on innovation.*

Goals For Americans, prepared at the direction of President Eisenhower in 1960, says, *"The magic ingredient is our competitive enterprise environment, the most powerful force ever known for stimulating individual and cooperative efforts to make innovations for the benefit of mankind. It encourages and rewards those enterprises which make successful changes, and punishes or eliminates the inefficient who fall behind."*

Relate, now, the business environment in which new commercial and industrial products are developed, with the environment in which new defense systems are developed. Don't the quotes above suddenly look "acceptable," when considering the nondefense nature of these products and enterprises?

Several points here are worth noting:

1. Development of new products, whether commercial or defense, is due to the same stimulus: competition. This competition comes from other companies, in the case of commercial/industrial products; and from other countries, in defense products. But in either case *competition rewards those who make successful changes, and punishes or eliminates the inefficient who fall behind.*

2. Most commercial products have a life span of only two to five years (there aren't many Wheaties developed, where Jack Armstrong never tires of them and neither will you). In contrast, a defense system such as the Polaris, B-52, or Minuteman is expected to have a life span several times as long—even though it is technologically much further advanced, relative to the consumer product, and more susceptible to technological obsolescence.

3. The average reader isn't particularly aware of and doesn't care much about corporate philosophy regarding new commercial or industrial products; but he is made aware in great detail, through news media, of what's happening at the Federal level of defense spending. This glare of publicity shines brightly, and often inaccurately, on What Will Make News Today. And "waste" makes news, even when it isn't really waste.

4. For every unsuccessful product developed, the chances are greater that future products will be successful because much is learned from the "failures." The B-70 and Navaho, for instance, contributed significantly to more advanced aircraft and to the rocket engines and inertial guidance of subsequent missiles, in the same way that commercial failures contribute to products that become successful. Failures are an inherent part of success.

"Corporate management, in considering the development of a new product, knows that a project requiring the least new knowledge, the shortest time, and the least financial support is probably going to be the least profitable, since competitors can be expected to have sufficient brains to follow along readily with their own versions. Experience has shown, also, that the converse is generally true. The more radical the idea, the longer the time, and the greater the financial risk, the better the chance for extraordinary profitability."[3]

In other words, the risk of failure is well worth taking in developing commercial/industrial products. The risk of going ahead with large defense systems, even with the much greater costs involved and the far greater technological risk, is at least as worthwhile because of the value of time, as discussed in Chapter 11. Unfortunately, it appears that the Pentagon's horns have been bashed in to the extent that it is pulling back to a "safe" posture on developments.

5. The $10 billion cost of cancelled programs, "slightly more than all the money the Government proposes to spend for education in the year beginning July," suggests mere elimination of programs that are cancelled, and presto! There's the year's education budget.

Education wouldn't get very far on this basis.

Some of the sixty-eight programs listed extend back over a period of *more than twenty years!* The beginning of Navaho and the B-70, the two biggest cancellations, go back more than fifteen years. If the $10 billion cited is prorated over an average of say, fifteen years, the cancelled programs average *less than 7 percent of the year's education budget*. This makes a rather dull comparison, however.

6. The cost of developing new commercial and industrial products that prove to be unsuccessful must be borne by the relatively few that *are* successful. The cost of these non-successes is paid for by the individuals in mini-skirt, slacks, uniform, tuxedo, and blue jeans who buy the successful items. These are also the same individuals who pay the taxes that provide the umbrella of defense that provides the opportunity for them to pursue their choice of livelihood.

7. It takes guts to cancel a program, to admit that it isn't going to live up to expectations. "To abandon in

midstream a cherished product idea which has already cost millions takes extraordinary courage, but companies are emphatic in saying that management must recognize the need when it arises and then act promptly and decisively."[4]

8. "It has been reported that 80 percent of new products introduced into the market by 200 large, well-managed companies have failed to return a profit,"[5] i.e., are unsuccessful *even after "deployed."* The odds may be considerably less. A Booz, Allen & Hamilton study shows that, on the average, only one new product idea out of forty is successful. Generally one in 100 is considered par. One authority says, "The odds that a product concept will be developed into a commercial prototype are about one in 100, and the odds that a product concept will become a commercial success narrow to about one in 1000."[6] It is impossible to *know,* before trying, which of these products will be the successful one.

Miraculously, critics of defense development expect a ratio of *one for one*—100 percent success! Where 1 percent to 20 percent success is par for new commercial or industrial products, these observers expect *infallibility* on weapons and support systems! "The military-industrial complex is hardly infallible." Nevertheless MIC is batting about .800, based on an annual RDTE budget (research, development, test and evaluation) of about $7 billion and allowing even twice the ballyhooed .66 billion dollars annual "waste."

9. The longer the development lead time, and the more the development effort approaches the featheredge of technology, the more likely it is that *wrong* decisions in product go-ahead will be made. In defense, the lead time is much greater and technology is generally far more advanced than in nondefense industries. The de-

fense products' batting average is therefore all the more remarkable, and the skill in organizing an effort of MIC's size and effectiveness becomes apparent. Decisions about defense projects are castigated by the underinformed—even though they're fully as sound as similar decisions in commercial and industrial businesses.

10. Incidentally, a comparison of the batting averages and costs of new products (defense vis-à-vis nondefense) reveals the extent of the "tunnel vision" with which some economists and other critics have abandoned objectiveness in order to attack defense expenditures.

11. One other point, and a major one, should be noted: *defense companies operate in a competitive, profit-oriented environment just as commercial companies do.*

Each category of industry is confronted with a cascading rush of new ideas from its competition, domestic and foreign. And the competitive pace in defense development is going to *pick up,* not diminish, whether or not we choose to stay in the race.

CONCLUSION

The American Marketing Association book says the first and most important decision in new products development is whether the organization has a strong enough desire to enter the prospective business area; whether it is willing to commit the necessary funds. The second decision concerns the organization and facilities required to develop and promote the project, including assignment of good men in a good working relationship.

MIC has good men, and it has a good working relationship. But as *Business Week* notes, "Today, the main threat to the security of the U.S. . . . lies in conflict and division at home;"[7] i.e., the organization known as America may *not* have a strong enough desire to enter the prospective area, although putting men on the moon indicates otherwise. As the '70s unfold, it may prove that the previous decade fielded men of greater daring and imagination. New products and new projects will take more time, more effort and money; and at the same time they will face shorter life cycles.

In space, defense, commercial, and industrial ventures, advancing into the unknown requires making a lot of what hindsight calls stupid mistakes. It takes guts to forge ahead, knowing "mistakes" are going to result in uninformed and unmerciful criticism, which may in turn cut off access to the creative minds required for meaningful research and development.

But the stupidest mistake would be to decide not to risk making mistakes.

4
How They Get Those Contracts

or

**HOW THE
OVERRUNS BEGAN**

"Such enormous rewards are conferred on a select few top companies at the whim of procurement officers: 86.4 percent of the $21 billion in contracts was awarded without competitive bidding."[1] Some of the terminology in this minor classic statement, noteworthy because it so concisely summarizes much of the misinformation on how contractors get contracts, deserves closer scrutiny.

☐ "Enormous rewards" apparently refers to enormous contracts. Any resemblance between the two often is purely coincidental. The C-5A program is an example of an enormous contract that produced not only *no* reward (other than in the way trial by fire builds character) but an actual loss. The real winner frequently is the company that can say, "Congratulate me—we didn't win!" Boeing and Douglas, in losing the all-out C-5A contest, avoided the great financial risk and harassment from Congress, DOD, journalists and other critics. "There, but for the grace of our

higher proposal price, go we." Particularly fortunate
was Boeing, who swung its development team almost
immediately onto the 747, an almost sure money-
maker.

☐ "Conferred" is a polite term for slipping the time
bomb to the "winner."

☐ "Whim" describes the hundreds or thousands of
man-days required for proposal evaluation and for
the myriad reviews and approvals required before a
recommended award is actually appoved. A typical
procedure for carrying out this whim is given in Appendix A, The Proposal Evaluation Process.

☐ A "select few" companies, such as General Dynamics, AT&T, Boeing, General Electric, Lockheed,
and others among the top one hundred defense producers, do, it is true, receive the largest contracts
(although they in turn subcontract more than 50
percent of these awards, including a large percentage
to small business firms). Should the taxpayer's money
be risked on companies that *don't* have proven management, *don't* have the high level of technical know-
how required, *don't* have adequate financing, *don't*
have the size to produce the hardware required,
don't have the necessary quality assurance capability,
and have never produced items of similar complexity?
If so, perhaps the C-5A or the F-14 or F-15 aircraft
contracts should be "conferred" upon The Jefferson
Airplane, which is suspected of being on the fringe of
MIC.

☐ Lockheed would probably be interested in knowing that it won the C-5A program "without competitive bidding," that, in the view expressed in the

statement above, Boeing and Douglas were merely going through a multimillion dollar exercise. The writer apparently has interpreted "negotiated award" as meaning "without competition." There's a vast difference between the two, as shown later in Chapters 6 and 9. *The competition on negotiated awards is usually more bloody than on advertised ones,* i.e., those open to all bidders. Perhaps the writer means "sole source award," which is a rare species used on small, proprietary study contracts and on modifications to existing contracts awarded as a result of competition.

Because of rampant misinformation on how companies get defense contracts and how cost overruns develop, it is worthwhile taking a look at how these contracts and overruns come about.

THE MARKETING GAME

You're in the role of "marketeer"/advanced systems representative/customer engineer (never "salesman," because that scares the customer, although in plain language that's what you are). There might not be anything on the shelf back at the store to sell because your company produces items according to whatever a contract calls for; nevertheless, you're a salesman because you're selling the customer on your company's capabilities, and you're feeding information on his up-coming requirements back to the plant in case the company wants to submit a proposal.

One day, unexpectedly, the mailman brings your company, Able Electronics, an RFP (request for proposal) to develop an electronic guidance miraculator. This project is something the company's engineers have wanted to do for a long time. After the decision to submit a proposal, the company becomes electrically charged itself. For several weeks the engineers talk excitedly, duck in and out of their cubby holes, and convene for conferences. Meanwhile the administrators, accountants, and publications people are waiting on one leg and then the other, crane-style, for the day when the engineers will finally release some proposal material.

The days and hours tick by, with the proposal effort rapidly approaching the due date. It's Lindbergh roaring down the runway on his takeoff for Paris . . . this is where he's supposed to take off, to clear the trees; but he/the engineers keep on going! The field is slippery and muddy—now they've roared past the "last chance for take-off" indicator! Pull up, engineers, *pull up!* They're still going full throttle, and the trees/deadline are almost impossible to clear. At the last possible second the engineers turn over the controls for incidentals, like getting off the ground, and in a frantic, round-the-clock all-out effort the pricing, photography, narrative, printing, and binding are rushed toward the deadline. The Spirit of St. Louis wobbles upward, one wheel brushing a treetop.

At 7 A.M. on the day when it's due, the proposal is finally wrapped and ready. But there's a hitch: it has to be delivered in Los Angeles and you, marketeer and delivery boy, are there with your package in upstate New York. Now begins another scramble: rush to the plane, which takes off in twenty minutes; transfer to another, and on across the continent. At the same time some six or eight other marketeers are also flapping their way toward LAX, each with a package of proposal documents in front of him. Onward roar the jets, bringing the competitors to the customer. You deliver Able's proposal with an hour to spare.

Thirty days later (this is a small one; therefore there's a fast reaction time) you get the word: do not pass go, do not collect contract, etc.

"How come?" You ask for a debriefing.

"Price too high; doesn't exhibit understanding of the problem," is the reply.

Conclusion: we've got to bird-dog the next one for *several months in advance* and get pricing to be more reasonable.

The next time around, the process starts with several months' advance tracking. Again the engineers are at the throttle, roaring down the runway; there is the last-moment liftoff—this time the price is competitive—and the flapping of wings toward the customer.

"Did we win?"

"Haven't completed evaluation."

Waiting, waiting, waiting.

"Sorry; you were close, but lost on technical; close on price and management capability."

Conclusion: those other guys were working on the proposal even before they got the RFP! So *that's* how the competition wins!

Third time around; flapping of wings. "Sorry, no award. Funds chopped."

Fourth round; going by habit now, like a fire horse. You keep hammering away, "We've got to get our prices down, you engineers and pricing troops!" But people are starting to give you funny looks, and they're asking, "When are you marketing guys finally going to bring in some business?" You begin to realize the proposals have cost the company quite a sum, like $30,000 to $60,000 per proposal. Comes time for the flapping

of wings, and the wait. Then, a phone call. They want to negotiate! Up, finally to bridesmaid! And that's all.

But the next time it's all the way up to bride. The sun is
finally out, the woods creatures are singing, there's joy in Mud-
ville. Sure the price was too low, and it will get smacked down
even lower in negotiations. But "We won it!" the plant rejoices.
(Win is we; lose is you.) The big boss pats you on the head and
says, "Go get 'em boy!" as he points you out the door again. But
the best part, music to the ears, is the competition mumbling
something about unfair competition.

Provided you and your company have the stamina,
money, patience, determination, capabilities, O.K. from your
new business committee, O.K. from corporate level for a too-
low price, and guts, that's how the marketing game goes. Without plenty of each of these your company should be in a different
ball game.

OPEN THE DOORS, GOVERNMENT

"Open up the game so that there will be more competition and lower prices!" This reasonable-sounding advice comes
from would-be competitors and from congressional observers
of military procurement. If ten competitors are pursuing an
award, isn't it more likely that the keener competition will result
in a lower cost than if only three or four are involved?

The problem is that it costs so much in a free enterprise
system to mount major proposal efforts. One of the costs is in
engineering talent; where only one company wins, the technical
effort of the losers is largely wasted. But proposals are expensive
in dollars too, to both the procuring Service and to industry.

In competition for the F-15 air superiority fighter, the
three finalists, North American Rockwell, McDonnell Douglas,
and Fairchild Hiller, each spent about $25 million of their own

money and the Air Force spent a similar amount. The competition started four years before award of the development and production contract, and toward the end of this period, North American alone had more than a thousand people involved in the proposal effort. The resulting volumes of proposal material exceeded that for the C-5A, when an airplane's worth of paper from each of the competitors descended on the Air Force evaluation team.

Another problem in opening the doors is that with contractors already being cited for too-low (unrealistic) proposal prices, broader competition will only aggravate this already sensitive condition.

Eventually the Government picks up the tab for higher general and administrative expenses (which include proposal expenses) of contractors who win. For those who lose, but whose general and administrative (G&A) expenses keep going higher because of the cost of proposals, the alternative is to submit higher (and therefore less competitive) proposal prices, or to get in another league where they can more effectively compete. Companies which have engaged in the torrid high-risk, high-stakes competition for defense contracts know that opening the doors wider for more candidates is doing no favor to those who think they *might* be able to win and *might* be able to perform on a resulting contract.

(Companies strive continuously to reduce the costs of proposal preparation. At an Eastern plant the controller was on a cost-reduction binge, particularly in regard to proposals, when a poposal with an expensive-looking and finely detailed cover design crossed his desk. Here was a horrible example of spending money on frills. "You see this cover?" he asked, jabbing at the offending item. "This is exactly what I mean about wasting money!"

The individuals around the conference table were silent for a moment. Then one spoke up, "But Alex, that didn't cost a cent. It was drawn by DaVinci."

"Oh yeah? Are you trying to tell me we've got a guy on the payroll who works for nothing?")

PROPOSAL EVALUATION

Meanwhile, back at the miraculator award, let's draw aside the curtain and look briefly at the process (whim, if you prefer) by which your proposal resulted in a contract award. (Chapter 8 gives an inside view of the award procedure in a Government procurement agency.)

After you dropped off the proposal package, shortly before the deadline hour, the proposal was logged in, and soon afterwards a team of professional procurement specialists under the direction of an appointed chief of evaluation (military or civilian) begins evaluating each of the proposals. Engineers analyze the technical content of each proposal (this is where Able's first two proposals were weak). Pricing specialists analyze prices on both a cost-by-item and a comparative-price basis. Management specialists analyze each company's management capability, as indicated by previous performance and how the company says it will go about meeting the time and cost requirements in producing the miraculator.

The assembled findings are then reviewed, and the Contracting Officer and a team of specialists negotiate price, terms, etc. with one or more companies. During these negotiations, often conducted simultaneously with the candidates, a price that was below rock bottom to begin with is smacked down still lower. At the same time, the Service may negotiate desirable technical features into the candidates' proposals. This obviously puts the competing companies in a very high-risk situation and contributes to likely overruns. (And yet, can the Services realistically be expected *not* to negotiate to the best of their capabilities, just to reduce the extent of an overrun?)

The recommendation of the proposal evaluation team (or that of the Contracting Officer, depending on the nature of the procurement) is reviewed by higher levels of authority. If they concur in the findings, your company will finally get a contract. Along the way, the agency's controller will have verified the availability of funds, and he earmarks the required amount so that the agency won't overcommit itself.

DEVELOPMENT OF AN OVERRUN

Let's look now at what happens inside Able Electronics after it has won the award for the advanced miraculator, in order to see how overruns, those infamous wreckers of fiscal budgets, develop.

In submitting their proposals, one bidder said, "Government, we can develop the miraculator for $7.2 million!"

"Our company can do it for six and a half!" claimed a second.

Able Electronics' internal estimate was $9.2 million. But the company figured it *might* be able to do it for less if the technical unknowns didn't prove too difficult. Able's proposal price was revised downward. "We can do it for $5.9 million— and in only eight months." Able's baby is a little faster.

In negotiations, Able's price went down to $5.2 million, on a cost-type contract (i.e., one in which most costs are borne by the Government. A little later, however, we'll see [Chapters 5 and 6] that the burden of risk has generally shifted to contractors.) Meanwhile you, the marketing rep, have headed out the front door and are otherwise engaged.

But back at the plant, the company starts to work. During the first month the project people get organized, Here's How We Are Going to Hack This Thing. The next month they start getting into the technical work and continue organizing. By now a lot of people are working on the project, and they're busy. But someone, probably the accountant-type on the project manager's staff, sees the costs going up and he pipes, "What happens later in the program, when we've spent the $5.2 million?" The reaction he gets is Back to Your Books, Accountant. This is a technical effort, and we don't expect *you* to understand the problem.

After about six months the engineers begin to understand the problem, and the solution they'd been knitting together starts to unravel. It's back to the old drawing board. The project manager (PM) calls the customer. "Say, you know the approach we've been working on, heh, heh? Well, we've got a new one that's much better. We'd like to brief you on it." The PM presents his case; but the uniformed customer has seen this kind of footwork before, and he smells an overrun building up. He controls his rage with difficulty. Finally he asks, "Will this have any effect on your price or delivery?"

"It probably will, somewhat. I'll get back to you on it."

The PM has his troops scramble to get a change proposal together. It turns out to be $2.8 million more than the original, and requires an additional six month's time. "We can't submit *that!*" he shouts. "Make it $2.3 million and five months." In negotiations it shakes down to $2.0 million, for a total of $7.2 million.

At the twelve-and-one-half-month point, the PM tells the customer, "You know, we may have been a little optimistic about that revision. It looks like it'll take another $2.2 million and six more months." The customer is ready to throttle him; but he's an officer and a gentleman, so he pins the PM to the wall with a scorching verbal blast instead. After the PM leaves, the customer sits alone at his desk, idly rubbing his neck.

Twenty months after The Day We Won the Contract, the Winner delivers, and the miraculator is *good,* even though "we underestimated it a bit." It wound up costing $9.4 million, just about what Able's original estimate was. Meanwhile the customer has shipped overseas and his successor is on the pan.

OVERRUNS: THE WINNERS AND THE LOSERS

This is how overruns develop: "chronic overoptimism" in proposal preparation; realization later of the cost/schedule facts of life because of better understanding of the technical problems; and a final price well above the original contract price.

There are no winners in an overrun. Able Electronics in this case might have earned a fixed fee, or profit, of 7 percent on the original $5.2 million, or $364,000. (If changes in scope of work to be performed had been directed by the Government, the Company would probably have received 7 percent fee on these changes also. As noted in Chapter 6, profit is recognized as the main stimulant to effective contract performance, as it is in any free-enterprise business. But the 7 percent would normally be reduced by nonreimbursable costs.) The company's management and stockholders would probably be embarrassed, in fact, at making this little profit on a $9.4 million effort, 3.9 percent before taxes, on the sales dollar.

But there are no real losers either in an overrun, provided the company exercises good business management. (The company could lose its corporate shirt, however, with overruns on an incentive contract.) If when you, the marketing rep, were flapping westward with your winning proposal, you and your Company had the foresight to *know* the technical problems involved, the exact manpower required, the exact time it would take for the breakthroughs required, and so forth, you could have come in with a proposal price of around $10 million, or about what the final cost turned out to be. But you would have lost the award and, more to the point, foresight isn't that keen. If it were, the customer could say, "You contractors *know* you can't do it for that! I don't want anyone to come in with a proposal of less than $9 million." The taxpayer and the defense procurement agency have received true value for their dollar; it's just that they, and the contractor too, hoped it would cost what the initial contract price indicated.

At the same time it's clear that overruns play havoc with fiscal planning and congressional tempers. One Senator charges, "They play games at the taxpayer's expense. We're being lied to!" in a mixture of pique and naïveté. If there's a culprit behind overruns, it's optimism; but without optimism, who—DOD, businessman, scientist, engineer, politician, New York Mets— would advance into the unknown?

CONCLUSION

This, then, is the process ("whim") by which a typical award is made.

It's not infallible, and there often are plenty of problems subsequent to making an award, such as the overruns that may develop. But the process is logical, involves reviews and approvals by professional specialists in the procurement business, and is well documented. (Maybe too well documented, in view of the costs of documentation; maybe not documented enough, considering the broadside of criticism levelled at MIC.)

Probably every award, however strongly justified, has second-guessers with reasons why it should have gone to some-one else. "Able shouldn't have gotten it because. . . ." And after an overrun develops, they will say, "I *knew* Able couldn't do it for that! It should have gone to Dog Electronics!" But the people at Dog aren't complaining. They know how similar the results would have been if they had won. They're thinking, "Thank God for Able."

5
How Much Money Is In It?

"Unconscionable Profits!" is the charge leveled at the defense industry by Senator McGovern of South Dakota (who claims for his state the distinction of ranking fifty-first among all the states and the District of Columbia in military prime contracts since 1967).[1]

It's unconscionable all right, others snap back; it's already well below what could be earned in nondefense work, and below what is required for the risks involved.

The profit outcry is something like a pie-throwing contest. It doesn't matter so much who throws first or whose aim is truest as which one makes the biggest splatter. The general impression of defense industry profits is reflected in this letter to the editors:[2]

War Profits Tax Hailed

A small but vital piece of information in *The (Los Angeles) Times* (May 28) referred to a bill proposed by Sen. George McGovern and cosponsored by

51

14 other leading Democratic senators, to place an excess war-profits tax of 85 percent on profits over $25,000.

This bill, long overdue, should not only be passed but made retroactive to 1965, when the great escalation in Vietnam led to equally great sums of money in certain pockets.

This would really cool the hot blood of our industrial war hawks.

Margaret Nolen, Laguna Beach

The McGovern bill was defeated, but Margaret's melody lingers on.

A tax on "war profits" would produce rather meager revenue. Lockheed, number two defense contractor, had a first-half profit in 1969 of only $17.5 million, on sales of $843 million. Boeing's first-half profits in the same period were $22.4 million, on sales of $1,531 million, most of which was in commercial sales. Both corporations' profits were down from the previous year. General Dynamics, number one in defense sales, had a $19.4 million loss.

If the point of the proposed tax was to punish defense producers, the tax was merely another blackjack blow on the noggin of an already pummeled industry. One wonders, "Well if they aren't making a hefty profit, why do they stay in this business?" It's a very good question. And the answer is a disturbing one.

DRAW FOR YOUR STATISTICS

The McGovern-Proxmire-Nolen complex has a Murray Weidenbaum study (by Prof. Murray L. Weidenbaum of Washington University, an economist and now Assistant Secretary of the Treasury) strapped to its hip, ready for immediate firing.

This study compares six relatively *unprofitable* commercial companies with six defense contractors of comparable sales volumes. The study's not-so-surprising results, in view of the commercial companies selected: the defense contractors earned higher profits. The quoters of this study overlook such factors as the extremely limited sampling involved, the fact that in two of the years excluded from the limited study (1960 and 1961) the defense firms lost money, and the fact that the study failed to separate the contractors' military and commercial businesses. "Details!" snap the McGovern-Proxmire-Nolen complex, which cites the study's figures as clear evidence that defense profits are higher than manufacturing's as a whole.

An exhaustive study of profits was made by the Logistics Management Institute, whose results are fired in return by MIC.[3] This study, covering ten years (1958-1967), is based on data obtained from forty companies having at least 10 percent of their business in defense sales, and a volume of at least $25 million or more in defense business. The data submitted by these companies was extremely sensitive and proprietary, and the results therefore provide considerable insight into profits, capital expenditures, and other data rarely revealed in highly competitive industries.

The Logistics Management Institute study compared operating results of these defense-oriented companies with 3,500 durable-goods manufacturers whose business is generally comparable (except in technology) and found that:

☐ Profit on defense sales ranged from 3.9 percent to 5.4 percent before tax during the ten-year period, whereas profit on sales in the general manufacturing companies ranged from 7.1 percent to 10.4 percent.[4]

☐ Profit on sales in defense companies declined more than 20 percent during the period, even though contractors' risks *increased*. It might have been expected that, with an increase in risk, profits would improve, rather than decline.[5]

☐ Defense companies are going increasingly into nondefense work; their commercial business increased *four times* as much as their defense work. General manufacturing companies' business increased more than twice as much as defense business.[6]

☐ Most defense business is 25 percent to 60 percent less profitable than defense companies' commercial business.[7]

"Yes, but look how small defense companies' investment is!" counter those who criticize profit on sales as a yardstick. "Their return on investment is far greater, because progress payments, government-owned facilities, and all those other subsidies enable them to get by with less investment."

Let's look at profit on investment:[8]

☐ Profit on investment (total capital investment; that is, equity and long-term debt) for defense business ranged from 12.2 percent to 20.4 percent before taxes.

☐ By comparison, profit on investment (total capital investment) for the 3,500 nondefense manufacturers ranged 14.1 percent to 23.1 percent.

☐ For the last five years of the study's findings (1963-1967), *profit on investment for the nondefense companies was 40 percent to 74 percent higher than for defense business.*

Aside from the results shown in the LMI study, the Proxmire group attack it on the grounds that LMI, a nonprofit organization established by former Secretary of Defense McNamara, is biased. This criticsm occurred to McNamara and his Defense Controller when the first LMI study was made. They had the results scrutinized for validity by an objective expert in finance at the University of Virginia Business School. It received loud and clear affirmation.

Nevertheless, the LMI study is continually shot at by Proxmire and his supporters, in spite of the wobbly underpinnings of their preferred study. An economist for the Proxmire committee even says, "Although no comprehensive study of such profits has been made, the known facts indicate that profits on defense contracts are higher than those on related nondefense business, that they are higher for the defense industry than for manufacturing as a whole and that the differential has been increasing."[9] It's hard to argue with some people; "Never mind the facts—our mind is made up!"

HOW DO PROFITS GET SO LOW?

Recognizing that not all observers believe that defense profits *are* low (e.g., to some, anything over $25,000 should be returned, 85 cents on the dollar, to the Government), the question pops up, how do they get so low? There are many reasons.

THE DIFFERENCE BETWEEN NEGOTIATED AND ACTUAL PROFIT

"If a company has damn good management," says a veteran Government procurement specialist, "it might make as much as 6 percent profit on a negotiated fee of 10 percent. But it takes exceptionally good management to make this 6 percent."

Negotiated or "going-in" fee (profit) gets sledge-hammered downward right away. (The highest allowable negotiated fee is 15 percent on a cost-type contract; in practice, negotiated fee is rarely more than half this percentage.)[10] One reason is that although interest is a normal business expense (and a substantial one, as the prime interest rate hits record highs), it is disallowed by the Defense Department as a recognized cost.[11] This cost, therefore, must come out of profits.

Another unallowable cost is advertising, except for "help wanted" advertisements. In every other kind of business, advertising is a normal cost of doing business; in fact, it's hard to do business without advertising. DOD says, however, "We aren't going to reimburse you for trying to influence us to buy," and therefore does not recognize advertising costs.[12]

Entertainment expenses are unallowable.[13] So are contributions, although companies are expected to contribute generously to the United Fund, Red Cross and other worthy organizations like good corporate citizens.[14]

Bad debts are incurred by almost every business; but these too arc an unallowable expense in the defense business.[15] The theory is that the Government is a good, reliable customer; contractors need not be concerned about DOD's credit. It pays. But payment isn't always made when due. In 1958, for example, the Secretary of Defense asked the defense industry to voluntarily delay billing the Defense Department because of the high rate of Federal expenditures at that time; and actual (if unrequested) delays in payment are not infrequent.

Losses on other contracts are not recoverable on a profitable contract." Each contract stands on its own."[16]

Business costs such as these are part of doing business in most industries, and they are recognized by the Internal Revenue Service as deductible expenses. But they're nevertheless not recognized as allowable costs by the Defense Department. Contractors understand the rationale behind DOD's position and have lived with these ground rules for years. The average citizen, however, and most writers on the military-industrial complex, are oblivious to these profit slenderizers. (For this reason, the basic rules of the procurement game are portrayed in Chapter 6.)

INCREASED RISK

The trend toward fixed-price contracts, and away from cost-type contracts, has shifted the burden of risk substantially from the Government to industry (although some commentators still talk about "low-risk defense business"). At the same time, competition for these contracts increased to this point: "For the overall firm fixed-price profit to sales ratio to be as low as it is, . . . Profit/Sales on price competitive, firm fixed-price business must be approximately zero." [17]

The effect of this increasing competition is a trend for the more-capable companies to leave the field wide open to the less-capable ones. After all, how can a contractor be expected to knock himself out doing a good job, if he earns zero profit? Nevertheless many senators and DOD officials unite in crying for "greater competition!"

INFLATION

The inflation each of us feels when checking out of a supermarket hits the defense industry particularly hard because of the sharp rise since 1965 in the cost of labor and materials. "Another cause of declining Profit/Sales . . . is the accelerated rate of inflation which has occurred in the last few years. Contractors undoubtedly underestimated cost increases which were to occur during contract performance."[18] This was a major reason for increases in C-5A costs, as noted in Chapter 2 and as acknowledged by both the Air Force and the contractor.

CONTRACTUAL FACTORS

Myriad other matters combine to reduce negotiated profits. One of these is "unbillables"—expenses incurred which are not billable to the customer. Changes directed by the Government customer, for instance, are not billable until covered by contract modifications; and the attendant delay is costly to the contractor. Another type of "unbillable" is *apparently*-requested changes. These are changes such as a customer's engineer might indicate as desirable and which are thereupon carried out by a naïve contractor. Later, when the contractor tries to invoice the customer, the customer says, "Oh yeah? Based on what contractual document?" There being none, the contractor swallows the cost himself, although he acted on what he thought (mistakenly) was an adequate directive.

Another type of exposure to losses occurs on a contract termination. The Federal Government is probably the only customer in the country who has the option of terminating a contract "for convenience"[19] as well as for cause. "For convenience" means that the Government can, without incurring a penalty, terminate at any time it wants. (Try *that*, on a private or business contract.) This is one of the ground rules in dealing with the Defense Department, and the reasons are sound: DOD doesn't want to continue buying an item, even though it has contracted to do so, if the requirement for the item ceases to exist.

In this situation, the Government agency responsible for the procurement will send the contractor a termination notice, requiring that he cease all work on the contract *immediately*. This means that he must cease both his in-house work and work being done by subcontractors. If he does *not* cease work immediately (i.e., by immediate action and telephone or telegram notice to subcontractors), the contractor himself is liable (out of his profits) for expenses incurred in grinding to a halt. [20]

THE MYTH OF THE PYRAMIDS

Occasionally someone will take a pot shot at "pyramiding of profits by subcontracting." Here's an example:

> Contractors often use Government-owned plants and equipment to produce defense goods; they typically receive payment for all costs incurred plus a generous profit percentage; and frequently they "pyramid" profits through subcontracting: a company granted the prime award delegates much of its work to other companies, which in turn delegate to subcontractors, and even, sometimes, through to sub-subcontractors. . . .[21]

The implication here is fuzzy. Perhaps this is criticism of a prime's making a profit on his subcontractors, whose price also includes a profit. It is hard to imagine that any contractor should assume the risks, guidance, coordination of effort and integration of subcontractors' efforts *without* having a profit (i.e., profit opportunity; actual profits may be slim or non-existent). At each tier of contracting a company is responsible for cost, schedule, and technical performance for not only the items it produces itself, but also for those it subcontracts. Typically 50 percent or more of a prime's program is subcontracted, in order to spread the workload and because a prime can't keep his people and facilities standing idle while waiting for receipt of a contract.

The implication may be that a prime might subcontract to a company which, in turn, subcontracts to a division or subsidiary of the prime's. In this case, doesn't the prime make *two* profits, one as prime and one as a sub-sub? Possibly, if the sub-sub can justify his price; but ASPR's control this. In addition, the Government contracting officer must be notified of the subcontracting structure, and must approve fixed-price subcontracts greater than $25,000, unless a purchasing system has previously been approved. These subcontracts are incorporated in a prime's subcontract, by reference to ASPR (Armed Services Procurement Regulation) 23-201, which regulates subcontracting.

A SWAMP NAMED COST PLUS PERCENTAGE OF COST

There aren't any cost-plus-percentage-of-cost (CPPC) contracts in the defense business. They are prohibited by statute. Nevertheless, occasionally someone will say in regard to defense contracts that the bigger the costs, the bigger the profit:

> Much is wrong with the peculiar system the Defense Department uses to negotiate the profits of its contractors, regardless of whether earnings turn out to be high or low. The main problem is that ever since World War I the Government has negotiated profit rates as a percentage of the contractor's costs.... Critics charge, justifiably, that the Defense Department's profit policy provides a perverse incentive to perform inefficiently. Because profits are computed as a percentage of costs, contractors are tempted to employ more engineering labor than is necessary.... [22]

En route from "here's what I think I've found out" to "here's how it is, reader" sometimes an informant gets bogged down in the cost-plus-percentage-of-cost swamp, unless he's familiar with the way businessmen normally figure their profit. In commercial, defense and industrial businesses, a businessman figures the costs of labor and materials; to this sum, he adds a percentage to cover overhead costs (which must be approved for defense contractors); to this total is added a percentage for general and administrative costs (again, approved for defense contractors); and then, when this total has been computed, a percentage for profit, such as 10 percent, is added. The total makes up the selling price for the item. This price is substantially "fixed"; and if at this price the businessman sells too few of the item to make money, his "profit" is actually a loss. If he sells enough beyond the break-even point to make a profit, fine. *But he has every incentive to keep his costs down* in either case. On cost-plus-incentive or cost-plus-fixed-fee contracts, as well as on fixed-price contracts, the defense contractor also has incentive to keep his costs down: return on investment, best use of hard-to-get skills, profit on sales, and reputation.

About the only throwback to CPPC contracts is in the commercial advertising industry, which prefers to think that its fee is computed on some other basis.

(The media department of a major advertising agency was asked whether it computes its fees on a CPPC basis. "Oh no! It doesn't work like that. We can place advertising at a 15 percent discount. For instance, if a television station were to charge you $1,000 for time, it would charge us only $850." [$150 is 17.65 percent of $850.]

When asked how the charge for preparing a commercial is figured, the agency's production department said, "Oh no! The way it works is that when we invoice a customer, we enclose the invoices of vendors to us, and add the 17.65 percent."

"Do other advertising companies charge in the same way?"

"I'm not sure, but I believe some may charge *without enclosing* the vendors' invoices. We don't operate that way, of course."

The advertising industry clearly has an eye that discerneth. To some, advertising's fee basis looks strangely like CPPC.)

THE PLUSES OF DEFENSE CONTRACTS

There are advantages in doing business with the Department of Defense that are uncommon to other types of business: progress payments, cost reimbursement on high-risk programs, Government financing for research and development, and use of Government facilities. Here too, however, there are a number of incorrect impressions.

PROGRESS PAYMENTS

". . . the big contractors hold most of the long-term, big-dollar contracts, the only ones that qualify for progress payments. . . . These liberal doses of interest-free money mean that the biggest suppliers furnish only about two-thirds as much of their capital as medium-size ones, and far less when compared with small contractors, who often get no progress payments at all." [23] The purpose and practice of progress payments clearly merits attention.

Contractors, large and small, frequently work to a schedule that provides for delivery many months after award of a contract. This may require *years* for a new ship like Litton's LHA or a new aircraft, such as Grumman's F-14. Meanwhile the contractor sustains a continuous outflow of funds for materials, engineering talent, overhead costs, interest, and other items. The purpose of progress payments is to enable the contractor, *whatever his size,* to perform on Government contracts which would otherwise be beyond his financial means.

But progress payments are no gift; and they include *no* part of the fee or profit earned. Typically, progress payments cover 75 percent or 80 percent of materials, labor, and manufacturing overhead costs already incurred.[24] The contractor must provide the remainder of these costs, as well as general and administrative costs; and he won't get progress payments at all unless he can show a need and negotiates these payments as part of the contract. There is no interest charge for these payments; but on the other hand neither does the Government, as pointed out, recognize interest costs as an allowable business expense.

Company size is not a criterion for qualifying for progress payments, but period of performance is: a contract must be of over six months' duration. The only way this might favor larger companies is that more of their contracts are long ones. But small companies also have contracts well in excess of the half-year's qualifying time.

USE OF GOVERNMENT FACILITIES

The Government long ago recognized that, realistically, industry had little incentive to put its own money into specialized plant and equipment for defense production, when the defense business is so accordion-like. Consequently, in order to have the capability of meeting emergency production requirements such as in a WWII or Viet Nam situation, the Government has extensive properties operated by the defense industry. But the extent is often overstated. It has been reported that the C-5A, for instance, is being built in a Government-owned facility; the truth is that half of the facilities are Government-owned and half Lockheed-owned. And the current value of the Lockheed portion far exceeds the Government's.

FINANCING FOR R&D

Because of the advanced nature of technology required in many defense systems, the Government encourages industrial R&D along these lines and pays for R&D performed under contract. This might be expected to yield commercial benefits for defense contractors. So far, however, the instances are rare where this kind of benefit has been realized. Generally the commercial market neither needs nor is willing to pay for the level of sophistication developed on defense projects.

COST REIMBURSEMENT

As previously mentioned, the burden of risk on development contracts has shifted from the Government to industry. There still are high-risk projects, of course, where advancing into the unknown requires cost-plus-incentive-fee contracting or, occasionally, cost-plus-fixed-fee agreements. Contracting is discussed in the next chapter. Generally, however, a contractor's neck is out a long way on cost-type contracts as well as on fixed-price ones.

PROFIT AS THE MARKET SEES IT

If one rejects both the Weidenbaum and LMI studies, the stock market is probably as good an indicator as there is for evaluating defense profitability. Most defense stocks sell at twelve times earnings or less, as compared to more than sixteen times earnings for the Dow Jones industrial average. In mid-1969 Lockheed's price/earnings ratio was 7.2; General Dynamics' was 11.4; Boeing's and McDonnell Douglas' were 10.2.

A *Business Week* summary of profits shows the aerospace industry as ranking near the bottom in profits in 1968 and

Profits lose some luster [25]

No. of Cos.	Industry	Sales 2nd qtr. 1969 [$000]	Percent change vs. 2nd qtr. 1968	Profits 2nd qtr. 1969 [$000]	Percent change vs. 2nd qtr. 1968	Profit margins	
						1969	1968
5	Aerospace	$ 2,416,351	− 7.0%	$ 72,722	− 6.0%	3.0%	3.0%
4	Appliance	386,686	+14.4	17,608	+37.2	4.6	3.8
13	Autos, trucks, parts ...	13,410,063	+ 0.3	724,719	−16.1	5.4	6.4
19	Building materials	1,038,783	+15.2	57,140	+13.7	5.5	5.6
23	Chemicals	5,171,837	+ 9.1	375,642	+ 5.1	7.3	7.5
8	Conglomerates	1,846,595	+ 1.7	78,824	− 5.9	4.3	4.6
6	Containers	1,454,088	+17.3	80,354	+12.3	5.5	5.8
8	Controls, instru.	416,108	+18.7	17,225	+22.8	4.1	4.0
6	Cosmetics, toiletries ...	816,797	+ 9.6	56,770	+12.1	7.0	6.8
19	Drug	2,327,579	+14.7	210,741	+12.7	8.2	9.2
14	Elec. equip., electronics	4,974,777	+ 6.3	194,826	+12.4	3.9	3.7
15	Food, beverages	2,583,698	+ 5.0	117,153	− 4.8	4.5	5.0
6	Glass	711,900	+10.0	48,782	+ 6.5	6.9	7.1
3	Hardware	105,292	+16.7	5,017	+93.6	4.7	2.8
18	Machinery	1,996,093	+ 6.8	123,766	+22.1	6.2	5.4
9	Nonferrous Metals	1,791,774	+11.1	150,849	+ 8.7	8.4	8.6
8	Office equip., Computer	3,125,628	+11.3	320,720	+13.5	10.2	10.0
17	Oil	5,770,959	+10.0	439,018	− 0.8	7.6	8.4
10	Paper	1,552,233	+ 7.5	90,636	+15.8	5.8	5.4
3	Photo equip., Optical ..	787,882	+ 7.3	102,498	+ 8.1	13.0	12.9
3	Plumbing, heating	176,361	+11.6	6,436	+56.8	3.6	2.6
5	Printing, publishing	319,678	+ 8.9	20,153	−13.1	6.3	7.8
4	R R equip.	408,011	+19.1	11,877	+35.2	2.9	2.5
8	Rubber	3,338,440	+10.1	151,819	− 4.0	4.5	5.2
1	Shoes, leather	89,523	+12.8	4,787	+14.1	5.3	5.3
19	Steel	3,127,433	− 7.2	158,806	−32.6	5.1	7.0
11	Textiles, apparel	1,319,024	+ 6.9	54,085	+15.5	4.1	3.8
2	Tobacco	590,645	+ 3.7	46,182	+ 5.5	7.8	7.7
7	Wood, wood prod.	1,585,901	+14.8	119,122	+28.1	7.5	6.7
37	Misc. mfg.	3,661,786	+ 9.3	205,884	+13.8	5.6	5.4
	Total	67,301,925	+ 6.0	4,064,161	+ 0.3	6.0	6.4

1969 among thirty major industries, *despite relatively good profits in these companies' commercial business.* Although a limited number of firms are included for each industry, it is clear from the size of sales that the largest in each group are included.

When commercial aircraft and other nondefense programs swing into full delivery, aerospace earnings and market prices will pick up. Meanwhile, bargain hunters aren't clamoring aboard aerospace or defense stocks' bandwagon.

RENEGOTIATION

If a contractor *could* make an excess profit, on whatever type of contract, he wouldn't be able to keep it. The Renegotiation Act of 1951 was designed to eliminate excessive profits from contracts and subcontracts related to national defense; these profits, where found, are returned to the Government. The Renegotiation Board found in 1956 that excess profits (before taxes) amounted to 51/100 of 1 percent of sales. In 1968, excess profits amounted to less than 6/100 of 1 percent of sales. [26]

CONCLUSION

"Unconscionable profit" depends on the eyes of the beholder.

"If there is a danger lurking within the business portion of the military-industrial complex, it may well be that defense will become so unprofitable that it is not worth pursuing at all."[27]

Dear Kindly Editor:

Some of my friends say there *isn't* any Santa Claus who passes out huge profits. I believe there is, and that he pours bags of money down contractors' smoke stacks. Please tell me, is there such a Santa Claus?

Virginia

Dear Virginia,

Your friends are right. But keep the faith, Virginia.

Kindly Editor

6
Rules of the Game

About the only thing the ASPR's (Armed Services Procurement Regulations) and *Playboy* have in common is the symbol of the rabbit. Other than that, they're miles apart, although 90 percent of the ASPR readers are red-blooded enough to peruse *Playboy* also. However harried, overworked, and tempest-tossed they may be, they usually find time to appraise at least the centerfold.

> Breathes there a man with soul so dead
> Who never to himself has said,
> "Hmm . . . not bad . . ."

The centerfold of ASPR 15-205, on the other hand, is a list of no-no's. ASPR's don't do much for tired blood.

ASPR's do have a way of multiplying like rabbits, however. From a standing start in 1947, they grew to a ten-pound volume in ten years, and now weigh about forty pounds, not counting the regulations of the individual Services. (The Army Procurement Procedures, Air Force Procurement Instructions, and Navy Procurement Directives total a hundred pounds or so, not counting the instructions developed by the Services' individual procurement agencies.) And the future promises even greater things; people who have never looked at the centerfold of an ASPR are demanding, "We need more procurement regulations!" These would require such niceties as complete subcontracting data and a requirement that contractors keep books and records on firm fixed-price contracts. This proposal, contained in *The Economics of Military Procurement,* could provide many times as much data as is now obtained for perhaps as little as $500 million a year. Millions for data, but not one more cent for defense, as we economists say.

Before the quagmire of regulations gets too sticky though, it's still possible to wade through an ounce's worth of procurement rules, dehydrated down to minimum weight, to get a basic understanding of the rules of the game.

There's obvious danger in swallowing a little bit of knowledge; but in view of rampant fantasies about cost-plus-percentage-of-cost contracting, generous profits, use of government plants, and progress payments to large contractors, exposure to an ounce's worth of rules isn't likely to add to the confusion. In fact DOD might well set up a "Rules of the Procurement Game" information shop, to shed light on fact and folklore.

WHO SETS THE RULES?

"Now, I'm coming in there with my *own* rules that you *must follow* when you play..." warbles Phil Harris in The Darktown Poker Club. This is the way with procurement regulations. The Government comes in there with its own rules that you *must follow* when you play. There's a regulation for practically everything: rules for awarding contracts, carrying out contracts, terminating contracts and rules for playing by the rules. Newcomers to the game are dazzled by the display. The producer of these ground rules is the Armed Services Procurement Regulation (ASPR) Committee, of the Office of the Assistant Secretary of Defense for Installations and Logistics.

RULES FOR AWARDING CONTRACTS

The basic policy of the Government is to award a contract to the firm which will supply an acceptable item at the least possible price and is responsive to the basic requirements of the request for proposal (RFP) or invitation to bid (IFB).

The Armed Services Procurement Act of 1947 provides that formal advertising is the normal peacetime procurement method, and that procurement by negotiation is the exception. Most contracts result from formally advertised procurements, where the lowest responsive bidder is, with few exceptions, the winner. Formal advertising is used if the item to be procured is standard; if it can be described by full and complete specifications; if there are a number of suppliers who want the business; and if adequate time is available for the procedures of formal advertising.

But often specifications are *not* clearly defined, or other reasons for formal advertising are not present, as in development of a C-5A cargo aircraft or an antitank missile where the specifications have to be developed. For this reason, and because of the increasing complexity and cost of defense systems, the *dollar value* of contracts placed by negotiation far exceeds the value of those placed by formal advertising, although these (negotiated contracts) are fewer in number. Critics of defense procurement practices continually refer to this disparity.

Negotiation, nevertheless, is the exception; and in order to purchase by negotiation, the Contracting Officer must draft a formal determination and findings (D&F) citing one of 17 specified exceptions to advertising, with justification for his recommendation. The D&F must normally be approved by the Secretary of his Service (Army, Navy or Air Force) or, in some cases, by the Secretary of Defense or the Bureau of the Budget. In addition, regulations require that the basis for selecting a research and development contractor must be fully documented. [2]

Procurement by negotiation does not mean there is no competition. On the contrary, competition often is fiercer than in formal advertising; and although *price* may not be the main factor on which the award is made (as it automatically is in advertised procurement), *value* generally is.

PROFIT AND FEE

In a contract resulting from formal advertising, the contractor's fee is presumed to be reasonable because of the competitive nature of the bids. In negotiated procurements, on the other hand, profit or fee is limited by law; and within these limits, the allowable fee is negotiated. In the case of a cost-plus-fixed-fee (CPFF) contract, the maximum allowable fee is 15 percent of the estimated cost. Weighted guidelines for setting profit and fee were developed during Secretary McNamara's tenure and are provided in ASPR 3-808, which recognizes profit as the main stimulus to efficient contract performance. In negotiating profit, the Contracting Officer considers such factors as the risks assumed by the contractor and his record of performance. Generally, a cost-plus-fixed-fee contract does not merit a reward of more than 1 percent for risk.

COST AND PRICE ANALYSIS

In formal advertising, simple price comparison of bids is usually sufficient to determine an award, without analysis of individual costs. (In Chapter 8, as you make decisions on advertised procurements, you will see this is not a mechanical process, however.)

In negotiated procurements, on the other hand, detailed cost analyses are made in order to compare the components of cost of one company against those of other companies, and against costs estimated by the procuring agency. These comparisons serve to detect inconsistencies in cost estimates (high or low inconsistencies), and ensure that each offeror understands what is involved in the Government's requirements. The Government procuring agency usually develops its own cost model during the proposal preparation time for familiarity with the proposals to be received and to evaluate proposal costs based on its own figures.

Having access to competitors' proposals and having developed its own cost model, the Government is well prepared for cost negotiations. In fact, the Services' negotiators can drive costs down to an unrealistically low level, although one of Secretary Laird's objectives is to reduce overruns.

TYPES OF CONTRACTS

ASPR 3-402 states in part:

Profit, generally, is the basic motive of business enterprise. Both the Government and its defense contractors should be concerned with harnessing this motive to work for the truly effective and economical contract performance required in the interest of national

defense. To this end, the parties should seek to negotiate and use the contract type best calculated to
stimulate outstanding performance.

Two principal types of contracts are used: fixed price
and cost types. If the contractor and Contracting Officer are
reasonably sure the item can be produced within the price
established by contract, a fixed price contract is used. If, despite the contractor's best efforts, the contract may not be fully
performed when the contemplated funds are expended, then a
cost-type contract is appropriate. The determining factor is
whether or not unusual contingencies are present.

Since the mix-sixties, fixed price contracts have been
used increasingly, and cost-type contracts less. The effect has
been a substantial transfer of risks from the Government to
industry.

FIRM FIXED-PRICE CONTRACT

This is the basic contract for defense procurement. It
is used in formally advertised procurements and in negotiated
procurements wherever possible. The firm fixed-price (FPP)
contract carries both the greatest possibility of profit and the
greatest risk of loss.

FIXED-PRICE-INCENTIVE CONTRACT

In this contract the contractor and Government negotiate a target cost, target profit, and ceiling price. By the terms of
the contract, the Government and the contractor share in the
difference between the target and actual costs; the effect is that
the contractor stands neither to profit nor to lose to the extent
he might under a FFP contract. An indication of the extent
to which risks have been transferred to contractors is the

fact that the C-5A contract is a fixed-price-incentive (FPI) one. Formerly this would have been a cost-plus-incentive-fee (CPIF) or even cost-plus-fixed-fee (CPFF) contract.

COST-PLUS-INCENTIVE-FEE CONTRACT

In a CPIF contract the Government and the contractor negotiate a target cost. Then they determine a target fee related to this cost and establish minimum and maximum fees, based on cost, schedule, and performance factors. If costs go up, for instance, the fee goes down. This type of contract is used where a cost-type contract is necessary and where its use will probably result in lower cost to the Government (lower than with a CPFF contract). The contract for developing the F-15 air superiority fighter plane is a CPIF type. (The production contract will be a FPIF type.)

COST-PLUS-FIXED-FEE CONTRACT

The CPFF contract provides for coverage of all *allowable* costs by the Government and a fixed fee to the contractor, regardless of whether these allowable costs are greater or less than estimated. The fee for performing a CPFF contract is usually only 7 percent. This dollar amount, less unallowable expenses, is "fixed," regardless of cost variances.

CPFF contracts are used infrequently now, but formerly were applied where a program involved high technological risk, as on spacecraft and long-range missiles.

CARRYING OUT THE CONTRACT

Regulations in carrying out the defense contract abound. Some, known as "boiler plate", pertain to requirements common to all contracts; others pertain to clauses such as financing that may be negotiated into individual contracts.

FINANCING

Paragraph 210 of Appendix E of ASPR provides that:

The need for advance payments or for progress payments or for a guaranteed loan (with reasonable
percentage of guarantee) shall not be treated as a
handicap in awarding contracts to those qualified
Contractors who are deemed competent and capable
of satisfactory performance. . . . A contractor deemed
reliable, competent, capable, and otherwise responsible, must not be regarded as any less responsible by
reason of the need for reasonable contract financing
provided or guaranteed by a Military Department.

Progress payments, discussed in Chapter 5, are one
type of financial assistance. The contractor's need, regardless
of his size, is the determining factor in allowing progress payments.

LABOR

A contractor is bound, by contract, to all sorts of labor
laws; and through him, his subcontractors are similarly bound.
These clauses are part of the standard "boiler plate" in a
contract. Some of these laws are the Davis Bacon Act, passed
to stop cutthroat competition in the construction industry; the
Walsh Healey Act, which provides for minimum wages, overtime, and standard working conditions; the Fair Labor Standards Act, providing minimum wages for employees engaged in
commerce or production of goods for commerce and a regulation that the contractor will not employ convict labor; the
Work Hours Act of 1962 pertaining to a standard work day
of eight hours and standard work week of forty hours; and the
Copeland or "Anti-Kickback" Act pertaining to construction

work. Government agencies and contractors are forbidden to discriminate against anyone on the basis of race, creed, color, or national origin.

Overtime work, except on firm fixed-price contracts, normally requires approval of the Contracting Officer or the Secretary of the Service concerned.

INSPECTION

Basic DOD policy on quality control is: (1) The producer is responsible for the control of the product quality. (2) The Government representative is responsible for determining that contractual requirements have been complied with, prior to acceptance. (3) Final decision of product acceptability is the sole responsibility of the Government representative.

The Government generally prefers sampling techniques rather than 100 percent inspection, since this provides the contractor with strong incentive to control the quality of his product; i.e., when total lots are rejected (as a result of sampling), the contractor finds much of his profit is lost by screening and reworking whole lots.

Some contracts have a latent-defect clause, in which defects found as late as six months and longer after acceptance are the responsibility of the contractor.

FACILITIES

The general policy of the Defense Department is that contractors will furnish their own facilities for performance of Government contracts. But in times of emergency, or in the development of a new item, it may be necessary that the Government provide facilities. In other cases, a prospective contractor is unwilling to risk his capital on a specialized facility, because no contractor can count on a continuing demand for the defense items which he produces.

Where a contractor requests the use of Government facilities, all costs connected with the use will be added to the contractor's base price for competitive evaluation purposes. Ordinarily when facilities are provided, their use is covered by a separate facilities contract.

SUBCONTRACTS

One writer (who apparently moonlights as a data processing salesman) says, "Strangely, in view of the high proportion of defense work that trickles down to subcontractors, the Pentagon does not collect overall data on subcontracting."

The subcontractor's legal relationship regarding his rights and duties is with the prime, not with the Government. If the Government were to begin acquiring the massive data inherent in subcontracting, it could find itself in the extremely awkward, as well as very expensive, position of relieving the prime *de facto* of his responsibilities. Overcontrol is already a continuing problem.

Fifty percent or more of prime contract awards is normally subcontracted, often through two or three tiers of subcontractors. The Government requires that prime contractors use the same procurement methods and many of the same clauses in subcontracting as the Government uses in placing prime contracts.

CHANGES AND SUPPLEMENTS

Changes to the contract may be directed by the Contracting Officer, as provided by the Changes Article of the contract:

If any such change causes an increase or decrease in
the cost of or the time required for the performance
. . . an equitable adjustment shall be made in the contract price or delivery schedule or both. . . .

In the past, particularly on CPFF contracts, contractors have often submitted low proposal prices with the likeli-
hood of increasing their revenue through changes.

DISPUTES AND APPEALS

Due to complexities in items procured and in the contracting process, disputes naturally arise between the Government and the contractor. The Disputes Clause in the contract
outlines the contractor's procedure in appealing a Contracting
Officer's decision. However, *"Pending final decision of a dispute
hereunder, the Contractor shall proceed diligently with the
performance of the contract and in accordance with the Contracting Officer's decisions."*

A dispute, if not resolved, may go to the Armed Services Board of Contract Appeals (ASBCA). This is an expensive and time-taking process, for both the contractor and the
procurement agency. Wherever possible they will generally
prefer to settle "out of court."

TERMINATIONS AND RENEGOTIATION

TERMINATION FOR DEFAULT

Terminations may be made by the Government for
default if the contractor fails to deliver within the time specified, fails to make sufficient progress, or fails to perform any
other provision of the contract. Before termination, however,

the contractor is given an opportunity to cure any default (except failure to make timely delivery). The Government wants delivery, rather than the problems connected with default.

Continual defaults by a contractor may make him ineligible to receive future Government contracts, subject him to excess reprocurement costs, and may subject him to damages. However, the contractor may claim that his default is caused by the failure of the Government to provide property or tooling on time, and this not infrequently is the case. The Government generally goes to great lengths to cure a default before taking default action.

TERMINATION FOR CONVENIENCE

The Government reserves the right to terminate contracts for its convenience *even when contract performance is satisfactory*. This is to protect the taxpayer and Government against paying for items under contract that are no longer needed. "Convenience" may be due to a cessation of hostilities, lack of funds, changes in requirements, or advances in weapons and equipment.

Termination regulations are complex, and Termination Contracting Officers who specialize in this phase are usually assigned to handle terminations.

RENEGOTIATION

During the Revolutionary War, General Washington suggested hanging of speculators who made excess profits. In the Civil War, fraud and corruption flourished in the absence of legislation on profiteering. In one instance, the Secretary of the Navy appointed an agent at a 2.5 percent commission to purchase ships for the Navy, when the going rate was 1 percent. The agent: his brother-in-law. In World War I, cost-plus-percentage-of-cost contracts were used, until the adverse incentive was recognized and fixed-fee and incentive-fee arrangements were developed.

In World War II, the Renegotiation Act of 1942 was designed to eliminate excess profits, and the Act has been extended and strengthened continually since then.

Prime contractors and subcontractors are subject to renegotiation if their contracts total more than $1 million in any one fiscal year. Excess amounts recovered in 1956 amounted to $152 million; in 1968, the amount was $23 million.

CONCLUSION

The rules of the Defense procurement game are complex and detailed; the brief summaries outlined in this Chapter are general, and there are numerous exceptions which are vital to the two parties involved.

But a glimpse of the bare essentials is necessary for an understanding of how the game works. That's what centerfolds are all about.

7
The Players

The players in the procurement game, on both sides of the fence, are about like their counterparts in any other game. Engineers, for instance, aren't bad guys; it's just that they talk funny and make funny marks on blackboards, like three sea horses and flat-shaped diamonds. Contracting people and purchasing agents, too, are fairly normal, although they talk in ASPRish and insist that everything be documented.

But there are differences between some of the people in the game and those who are not in the game. In order to know something about the players, it's necessary to take a brief look at the program. More fundamental than that, it's necessary to look at the team captains and to see whether there is an underlying philosophy that guides them and, in turn, their teams.

MEMBERS OF THE TEAM

In addition to the specialists, there are a great many people in administrative and support roles who make up the contractor's organization and the Government procurement agency's organization. As in other enterprises, people are the main asset in accomplishing the organization's purpose.

ENGINEERS

There are practically all kinds of engineers in defense procurement—guidance and controls engineers, aerodynamicists, propulsion engineers, and design engineers of all species. About the only kind not included is Engineer Bill, who carries a long-stemmed oil can and wears a peaked cap. Each breed of engineer has its own jargon, but there are similarities between the various types. They never want to consider a job finished, for instance; they have to be pried, like abalone, from infinite engineering. Engineers eat like lumberjacks, particularly when the company is picking up the tab. The same skills and appetites are found on both the industry and Government sides of the fence.

ACCOUNTANTS

Accountants, too, are found in abundance on both sides. Some wear the usual thick glasses, dark suits and look as though they need a square meal; but they don't fall into patterns as neatly as do engineers. Accountants talk about G&A rates, tab runs, and allocable costs. When others refer to $5,969.83 as six thousand bucks, for convenience, the accountant talks about it as five thousand, nine hundred sixty-nine dollars and eighty-three cents.

LAWYERS

Attorneys on both sides give legal opinions regarding contemplated decisions and, generally, their necks are well in.

But they were picked up in the sights of one writer who describes the military-industrial complex as a "crew of military contractors, generals, public-relations scalawags, military associations, professors and scientists, congressmen, lobbyists, unions, and general riffraff of local Chamber of Commerce secretaries, *lawyers,* and the like."[1]

There's a need for this legalistic "riffraff" because the rules of the game, voluminous though they are, leave considerable latitude for judgment on the part of Contracting Officers and other decision-makers. In fact, the game is played on a big playing field broken only occasionally by trees represented by ASPR's. The players rarely crash into an ASPR, because both sides know the ground and the ground rules. Where they collide is at the judgment points, which may occur anywhere on the playing field. These collision points are where the lawyers are needed.

MARKETEERS

These individuals are found only on the industrial side, and we have seen something of their duties and functions in Chapter 4. Marketeers tell customers how great their company is, attend conferences, glean information on forthcoming procurements, and travel a lot, usually on a night plane called The Redeye.

CONTRACTING OFFICERS/ADMINISTRATORS

Contracting is the heart of the military-industrial complex because of complexities of the rules and the items procured, and because most items must be produced to a contract, rather than purchased off the shelf.

Contracts administrators on both sides of the table carry out the bulk of contractual matters; many are lawyers.

The Government Contracting Officer is the focal point in awarding and administering contracts. He's really about forty people, because contracts administrators, engineers, procurement specialists, buyers, and others represent or advise him on procurements. But he alone is responsible, and he bears the authority and responsibility for seeing that the Government gets its money's worth. Decisions involving technical problems, schedules, costs, people, and legal aspects are his to make, correctly.

QUALITY ASSURANCE SPECIALISTS

Specifications are extremely tight on military contracts. Inspectors can exercise judgment to a limited degree on what's acceptable and what's not, but they generally go by what the specs call for. If a decal is supposed to be in a certain position and affixed to equipment in a certain way, they aren't likely to allow deviations, regardless of how perfect the complex piece of hardware is that bears the decal.

Because meeting requirements is necessary before the Government accepts an item, and because a contractor can't receive his profit until this acceptance, the contractor has his own quality assurance specialists whose function is to catch deficiencies and ensure corrections before the Government inspector does.

OTHER PLAYERS

There are numerous other players—plant representatives, pricing specialists, small-business specialists, contract modifications specialists, industrial mobilization specialists, finance specialists, and others—and each fills a need in the field of industry or Government contracting.

THE ENVIRONMENT

Are these people capable? Are they ambitious? How hard do they work? What incentive is there to do a good job? Why do they stay in this business?

These are professionals, mostly people with degrees related to their specialties. Many have advanced degrees. Pride in their work and desire to use the capabilities they have are two of the reasons they do a good job. The industrial side is paid perhaps 5 percent to 10 percent better than counterparts in commercial industry; but over the long run, an individual probably receives about the same remuneration in either category.

One of the frustrations in the defense industry is the effect of rapid changes. When a program is completed, a company lays off everyone it doesn't need, and these individuals then scramble for spots with other companies whose programs are "phasing up." Over a period of years an individual comes to belong more to an industry than to a company, and in the process of his moves he usually loses the retirement benefits that would accrue to a lesser-paid individual in non-Government industry.

A continuing hazard, to technical people at least, is that their skills become obsolete or obsolescent about every five years. This means going to school, on either a full-time or part-time basis. Often their companies pick up part of the tab; but the individual must invest his own time in order to stay proficient in his field.

Most of the contracts people, accountants, controllers, and other specialists also continually upgrade their professional skills. They have to, because of the competitive nature of the industry and the challenge from the Other MIC, the U.S.S.R.

These skilled people don't always stay in the defense business, of course, and their skills often make them highly desirable to other industries, such as oil and communications. About every five or six years, when there's a shake-out in defense spending, some of the most capable people leave. Two or three years later, when an international crisis comes along, contractors plead with qualified people to return. The accordion's tune was ever thus.

MORALE

The people on both the Government and industrial side of MIC are sincere, capable, and dedicated—like other groups of professionals. They're hardworking, under tremendous time pressures, and confronted with the most difficult challenges of technology and production.

And like other individuals, they aren't indifferent to praise or criticism. If they were hippies or playboys, maybe they could care less whether anyone recognized or appreciated their efforts. But these are people who work, and their morale, high or low, affects their work.

An eighteenth century French philosopher said, "To destroy a man, it is necessary only to give his work the character of uselessness." Most reasonable people don't mind being criticized if the criticism is just. But the wave of criticism directed at MIC is often based on incorrect information, misinterpretation, lack of knowledge, and news value. For the most part, it reflects national frustrations over unrelated or remotely related events. But the MIC professionals, high and low, aren't blind to the fact that this criticism overlaps into personal attacks and pinpricks.

It sometimes becomes awkward for a man on a Government program to explain to his relatives, his children, and maybe his barber, that he and his company are doing a good job when only the shortcomings of his program are publicized. A neighbor might say, "Well, I see you've wasted another $2 billion of taxpayers' money." On one program where the people produced a superb product and thought they had done a highly commendable job, their performance was so severely criticized that morale plummeted and productivity dropped 40 percent.

Related to this is the problem of recruiting good people, in both Government and industry. A certain amount of criticism is always healthy. "But the same rules should apply to political criticism that apply to big-game hunting. You don't hunt so hard and shoot so murderously that you wipe out the breed. . . . It's time that we took some elementary conservation measures."[2]

LEADERSHIP

Many of the same factors are present on either side of the fence in the procurement game: constant personnel changes, changing requirements, fast starts and stops depending on budgets and technology, a tough set of rules, tough specifications, openness to audit and hindsight, and the glare of publicity. Providing the equipment and services needed for defense requires a high order of leadership, in view of the large, complex, difficult nature of the game.

Although earnings figures don't show it (and that's how quality of leadership is often judged in business) leadership in defense companies is usually top-notch compared with others of comparable size. It may be even better than that, considering the parameters in which it operates.

But earnings are only one measure of achievement. This same leadership has accomplished considerably more:

> In the mighty and almost limitless potential of American industry, the brilliance and rugged determination of its leaders; the skill, energy and patriotism of its workers—there has been welded an almost impregnable defense. . . . It is indeed the most forceful and convincing argument yet evolved to restrain the irresponsibility of those who would recklessly bring down upon the good and peace-loving peoples of all the nations of the earth the disaster of total war.[3]

DUTY, HONOR, COUNTRY

What is it that keeps these people, these leaders in industry and in Government, going in the loneliest war? Is there a philosophy that leads them onward, something that causes them to dedicate themselves to what they're doing, something they see that others don't, something that keeps them heading toward a purpose in spite of abuse and attacks?

Yes, there is. It's not just the standards of conduct, although it is necessary that these be outlined, as in this excerpt from a letter by a chief signal officer, which is typical of instructions to Government personnel:

> The necessity for maintenance of the highest standards of conduct by . . . personnel engaged in procurement and related activities is a continuing one. Constant vigilance is required on the part of each individual to safeguard the reputation of (the Service) for honesty, courtesy, and fair dealing in its relations with contractors. Integrity and straight-forwardness in conduct is a way of official life, as much

to be desired as in private life. Every commander and every supervisor has the opportunity, and the additional obligation, by precept and example, to exercise leadership in this field. . . .

And the philosophy is only partly reflected in this comment by the chief executive of the number one defense contractor: "I don't care about what I'm being called now. But I don't want anybody in 1979 to say, 'Why didn't the professionals do their job in 1969?' "

The spirit that guides these team captains in industry and in the military was best stated by an American, speaking to a group other than MIC, who foresaw a time when politicians would impugn the integrity of individuals in uniform and business suits; when professors and other pedants would mimic and deride Americans who live by a creed of honor and service; when magazines and their cartoonists would belittle leadership with mockery and ridicule. In an extemporaneous speech (reprinted in full in Appendix B) this American, Douglas MacArthur, said:

> Duty, honor, country: Those three hallowed words reverently dictate what you ought to be, what you can be, what you will be. They are your rallying point to build courage when courage seems to fail, to regain faith when there seems to be little cause for faith, to create hope when hope becomes forlorn. . . .
>
> The unbelievers will say that they are but words, but a slogan, but a flamboyant phrase. Every pedant, every demagogue, every cynic, every hypocrite, every troublemaker, and, I am sorry to say, some others of an entirely different character, will try to downgrade them even to the extent of mockery and ridicule. . . .

Yours is the profession of arms, the will to win, the sure knowledge that in war there is no substitute for victory, that if you lose, the nation will be destroyed, that the very obsession of your public service must be Duty, honor, country.

Others will debate the controversial issues, national and international, which divide men's minds. But serene, calm, aloof, you stand as the nation's war guardians, as its lifeguards from the raging tides of international conflict, as its gladiators in the arena of battle. For a century and a half you have defended, guarded, and protected its hallowed traditions of liberty and freedom, of right and justice.

Let civilian voices argue the merits or demerits of our processes of government: whether our strength is being sapped by deficit financing indulged in too long, by Federal paternalism grown too mighty, by power groups grown too arrogant, by politics grown too corrupt, by crime grown too rampant, by morals grown too low, by taxes grown too high, by extremists grown too violent; whether our personal liberties are as thorough and complete as they should be.

These great national problems are not for your professional participation or military solution. Your guidepost stands out like a tenfold beacon in the night: Duty, honor, country.

You are the leaven which binds together the entire fabric of our national system of defense. From your ranks come the great captains who hold the nation's destiny in their hands the moment the war tocsin sounds. . . .

The long gray line has never failed us. Were you to do so, a million ghosts in olive drab, in brown khaki, in blue and gray, would rise from their white crosses, thundering those magic words: Duty, honor, country.

This does not mean that you are warmongers. On the contrary, the soldier above all other people prays for peace, for he must suffer and bear the deepest wounds and scars of war. But always in our ears ring the ominous words of Plato, that wisest of all philosophers: "Only the dead have seen the end of war."

8
The Game:
First Half

Robert Immel was on the phone, from New York. Robert Immel, President of Atlantic Coastal Industries (actual names are disguised), was not happy.

"Yeah, you guys up there in your ivory tower—you like spitting down on us contractors from your fifteen-story office building, don't you?" Three individuals in a government procurement agency were on the listening end, on the fourteenth floor of the former Penn Athletic Club building. Immel began to warm up to the subject, spewing out years of apparent poison triggered by the Contracting Officer's awarding a contract to another company. Most of it was aimed at Sam Rabinowitz, civilian Assistant Chief of Procurement, some at the agency's chief engineer, and the rest at Stan Johnson, the Contracting Officer.

Some of Immel's kinder expressions were, "Crook . . . shyster (Sam was a member of the bar) . . . bastards . . ." in what turned out to be an hour-and fifteen-minute toll call. The

Contract Officer got a couple of chances to say, "Mr. Immel, I'm the one who made the award . . ." but Sam was the primary target, along with the agency and the U.S. Government in general. About midway through the monologue Johnson squeezed in, "Mr. Immel, we're beating a dead horse; the award has been made. . . ." More verbal brickbats at Sam. Only he knew how many times he'd been through similar situations.

Eventually Robert Immel concluded with an abrupt, "You guys in your ivory towers—I'm going to my Senator and my Congressman, and you haven't heard the last of this!" (Immel's complaint resulted in an investigation by the General Accounting Office (GAO), whose initial conclusion was that a mistake had been made in the award. Evidence substantiating the Contracting Officer's decision caused GAO to reverse this conclusion, however.) Then with a bang, Robert Immel hung up. Maybe he just hadn't wanted to go home late that Friday afternoon.

Magazines and newspapers that talk about Government-industry footsie and the "murmuring of lovers" don't know about Robert Immel down there at street level, dodging spittle and yelling a stream of endearments at the fourteenth floor.

The Contracting Officer is at the point where a pyramid of contractors, all with razor-sharp individual interests, meets the inverted pyramid that is the Government, with its audit agencies, accounting offices, review boards, and so forth. He's right at the point where the best interests of the country, with him as its representative, meet the profit motive, the point where the Government gets its equipment or services and the contractor gets his money. This is the working level, and here, rather than at the higher administrative or policy levels, is where the real action is. Contracting, it turns out, is jumping on the fire engine and roaring off to the fire; or Cowboy and Indians, and your scalp is the objective.

THE GAME

Assume that you're a Contracting Officer (C.O.) in a Government Procurement Agency of several thousand people. Most are civilians, although some are military. Your guiding principle in contracting for military equipment is simple: do what is in the Government's best interests.

Reporting to you are about thirty engineers, purchasing agents, and other specialists. Other people, including lawyers, pricing specialists, production and facilities specialists, and quality assurance personnel, are available for support as required. You are at the center of the decision-making process in an organization that looks something like this:

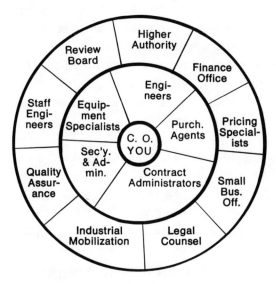

Figure 1.

This chapter is arranged differently from the others in order to give you a chance to make decisions without the glare of adverse publicity or the burden of explaining your actions. You probably won't need to read all the pages, if you make correct decisions, and if you follow the directions.

As in actual contracting, there is always time pressure. You should make the decisions and complete this chapter in sixteen minutes. Remember, time is money; but more important, time means getting equipment in the hands of the using Service as quickly as possible.

FIRST DECISION

A procurement directive is received in your agency requiring the procurement of a large quantity of housing units. These are aluminum shelters like campers that will be mounted on the beds of trucks, each to be used for housing radio equipment and two or three operators. The units are a production item, and no development is required.

In response to the invitation for bids (IFB) sent out by your agency, eight bids are received. All bidding companies appear to be qualified and responsive. But there is an unusually broad range in their prices:

Bidder A	$2,800 per unit
B	3,900
C	4,150
D	4,200
E, F, G, H	4,600 to $5,800 per unit.

It looks as though Company A might possibly have made a mistake in its bid, in view of the closeness of the other's prices. Which one of these three actions do you take?

Make award to Company A—see ①, below.
Make award to Company B—see ②, page 100.
Take some other kind of action—see ③, below.

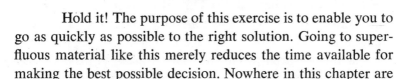

Hold it! The purpose of this exercise is to enable you to go as quickly as possible to the right solution. Going to superfluous material like this merely reduces the time available for making the best possible decision. Nowhere in this chapter are you directed to this section.

Now go back to page 98 and make a decision.

①   You decided to make the award to Company A—and this looks like the best interests of the Government, since A's price is considerably less than the others. If he's too low, that's his tough luck; you can stick him with it.

But it's strange that the others are grouped around such a narrow margin ($3,900 to $4,200, for B, C and D). And what if it turns out that A misunderstood and can't produce? In that case, you'd probably run through six to ten months with him; find that he's going (or gone) broke; and then would have to start all over again, probably going with B. Meanwhile, though, B's price would certainly have gone up, and he may not be interested in the business at that time.

If you stick with Company A, see ③, below.

If you decide to go with Company B at this point instead of Company A, see ②, page 100.

③   You're doing fine! Company A looks like the winner, but you need to be sure that he understands what's involved in the housing unit, and that he has the finances, people, facilities and capability to produce.

So you decide to send an evaluation team up to his plant to verify these things—that's what some of the support people are for. In three days you have their written report: financial strength O.K., production capability O.K., quality assurance O.K., and management ability O.K. It turns out Company A's main line of business is making tollhouses for toll parkways, and the housing unit is similar in size and manufacturing processes to what they've been producing. They'll have to expand their capacity somewhat, but they have a plan and the resources to do this.

With the evaluation team's report, you decide: go with A. You therefore ask the head of the Review Board, a senior civilian in the agency, to schedule a meeting of the Board. He sets a time for 9:00 A.M. two days from now. The purpose of the Board is to analyze your recommendation, and in turn to recommend approval or disapproval.

At the appointed time, you and your purchasing agent appear before the Board (composed of legal, production, pricing, engineering, and other senior specialists) and present your recommendation. The proceedings are recorded on tape, and the Board members try to pick apart your analysis and conclusion. If your decision stands up, the Board's recommendations and yours go to higher authority for approval. If it doesn't stand up, you'll have to do a better analysis, or reconsider your decision.

Now see 4, *page 101.*

———————————⭐———————————

2   You decided to make an award to Company B, probably for the reasons that B and higher bidders *must* understand the requirement better than A, whose price is almost 30 percent under B's. A's bid, in fact, seems to cover only the prime costs—material and labor—that B's bid calls for, as analyzed by your engineers and purchasing agent. There are good reasons, therefore, for selecting B.

But you'd be shot down by the Review Board, and you know too that your conclusion, without further checking, would cost the U.S. $1,100 *per unit* if your recommendation is wrong. You don't have enough information at this point to make a determination.

Therefore, see again ③, *page 99.*

If you first chose Company A, and then decided to go with B instead, remember that the premium is not so much on *whom* you recommend as why. Your recommendation will have to bear intense current scrutiny, and it will be subject to review for *years* into the future. You can get all the support you need, within reason, for information gathering; but the decision-making responsibility is yours alone.

––––––––––✪––––––––––

④　　Later in the day after the Review Board meeting, your phone rings. The Chief of Procurement for your agency is considerably disturbed about your recommendation of Company A. "How can they possibly do it for this? Why, their price per unit is only what the others' *prime costs* come to!" He can visualize the award coming to a reprocurement situation within a year; and meanwhile the units are badly needed.

You go over again the reasons for your decision and the evaluation board's findings; and as you hang up, you recognize that, with his experience, the Chief might be right. Time will tell, when Company A's first delivery date is due. You begin to feel a little lonely.

Should you have tried to get the Chief's opinion before making a recommendation? Should you have canvassed the members of the Review Board immediately, and then made a decision?

No. The surest way to go wrong is to try to please everyone who reviews your decisions. Contracting isn't a popularity contest; it's a matter of judgment and the guts to stick with a decision regardless of who attacks it, if you're convinced it's sound. Your guiding principle is very simple: do whatever is in the best interests of the Government. You'd never be able to please everyone anyway.

Time pressure is intense, however, and it's necessary to make decisions quickly and right. Wrong decisions are quicksand; the time it takes to rectify them leaves less time for making right ones, in real-time situations.

SECOND DECISION

Because of heavy rains and landslides, a Western area of the country has been declared a disaster area. To help alleviate economic conditions there, your agency has asked for proposals on certain items from firms in this area. Your agency is not too familiar with some of the firms solicited, but has been directed and wants to assist in the purposes of disaster relief.

In response to a request for bids on a remote control unit (used for operating communications equipment from a distance, so that if a mortar or artillery shell drops in on the equipment, it won't also get the operators), one of the firms in the disaster area comes in with a bid of $1100 per unit. The next bidder's price is $1700 per unit.

This looks like another low-price/can-he-or-can't-he decision.

Because of the time and distance involved (and travel expense), you try to verify, by phone, that the company understands what's required. You ask your administrative chief, Stu Blane, to make the call.

"Hello, Pacific Electric? This is the Procurement Agency on the remote control competition. Is the company President there?"

It turns out he's in New England on a business trip, but the company's chief engineer is there. He gets on the phone.

"This is Stu Blane on the remote control unit. I just wanted to call and verify a few things about your bid." Stu doesn't want to ask outright whether the company bid too low; so he asks things like the company's size, financial status, engineering and quality assurance capabilities. Then he comes around to price and delivery. "By the way, I've looked over your cost breakdown and price. I presume you analyzed these carefully in preparing your bid. You're quoting $1100, right?"

"Right," the company's engineer says. Stu groans internally, and winds up the conversation with, "Okay; we'll be in touch with you."

Stu reports his conversation to you, the C.O., and writes a memo for record on the conversation. What do you do?

Try to contact the company President—see ⑤, *below.*

Go to the Review Board with a recommendation for Pacific Electric—see ⑥, *page 104.*

———————⭐———————

⑤ You decided to contact the company President who's in the East. If it turns out the bid price is correct—that is, if the President verifies it—fine. But if for some reason there's a mistake in the bid, awarding it to Pacific Electric may *add* to the disaster, rather than alleviate it, as well as causing delay in getting the remote units.

Therefore, you contact the company and ask them to have their President, John Talley, get in touch with you.

Later that day he calls you from an Eastern city. He sounds distressed, and indicates there's been a mistake in the company's price estimate. He wants to see you the next morning.

What should you do:

Agree to see Talley, and consider a price change from him?—see ⑦, *page 104.*

Tell him you're sorry, the bids are closed and you'll be glad to see him, but no changes will be considered?—see 8, *below.*

Agree to see him, and consider letting him withdraw his bid?—see 9, *page 105.*

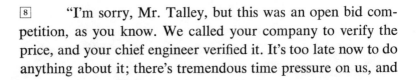

6   If you go to the Review Board at this time, one of their first questions will be, "How do you know they can do it for this price?" You have the company's chief engineer's verification; but you and your agency don' know his or the company's capabilities very well. If the engineer is wrong, he's out of a job; but his company may be out of business. Remember, your guidance is what's in the best interests of the Government, and the Chief Executive has declared the region a disaster area. You need to be sure that you wouldn't be *adding* to the disaster by awarding a loss contract.

Return to page 103 and choose the other alternative.

7   If you agree to see the President, you can hardly let him raise his price; this would prejudice the other bidders. He could, for instance, raise it to $1695, or just below the next bidder's price of $1700 (this is open competition, and prices are made public as soon as bids are opened). Therefore you decide that this course, which Talley might propose, is out of bounds.

See 8, *below.*

8   "I'm sorry, Mr. Talley, but this was an open bid competition, as you know. We called your company to verify the price, and your chief engineer verified it. It's too late now to do anything about it; there's tremendous time pressure on us, and

it's already in the approval process. I'd be glad to talk with you about it. Maybe we can suggest sources where you can get any additional assistance you need. The Small Business Administration, for instance, might be glad to help."

If this is your response, it's a safe and easy way out, for now; but it could turn out to be a tremendous time-waster. The company almost surely would lose money, and the Government very likely wouldn't get its equipment. This costs the Government doubly: it wouldn't get the items it needs and it would in effect be responsible for causing the company to go under.

See 9 , *below.*

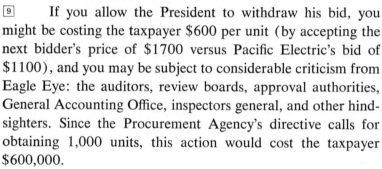

9   If you allow the President to withdraw his bid, you might be costing the taxpayer $600 per unit (by accepting the next bidder's price of $1700 versus Pacific Electric's bid of $1100), and you may be subject to considerable criticism from Eagle Eye: the auditors, review boards, approval authorities, General Accounting Office, inspectors general, and other hindsighters. Since the Procurement Agency's directive calls for obtaining 1,000 units, this action would cost the taxpayer $600,000.

You agree to see him; and when he comes in, Pacific Electric's President is shaking like a leaf. It turns out his chief engineer prepared the bid in his, Talley's, absence, and it is about 50 percent too low.

You decide to let him dangle a little. "Aside from that, Mr. Talley, how's your production capability? How much would you have to enlarge your facilities?" It turns out four times. "How about financing; can you get loans or financial backing for performing the contract?" He shakes more visibly, but believes he could. "How about people—any trouble in getting and training the production people and quality assurance and others required?" No . . . his voice trails off.

"Well, Mr. Talley, it looks to me as though you might have some trouble performing on the contract, in view of all the changes you'd have to make to get ready. What do you think we ought to do?" He doesn't know.

"We might consider allowing you to withdraw your bid, if it's something *you* want to consider." The dying man grasps at the straw. He recovers enough to dictate a letter asking that his company's bid be withdrawn. He shakes hands weakly and walks out, still trembling.

He has no idea how glad *you* are that he took this action. You document the situation with a memo for record. You'll need it for the Review Board, and later.

Your neck is out, however; it could always be said that you cost the Government $600,000 by allowing this action to be taken. "How do you *know*, C.O., that he couldn't have produced?" And you don't *know,* because you didn't award the contract to Pacific Electric. All you have to go on is the facts and your judgment.

THIRD DECISION

Let's try another example.

You're now an Administrative Contracting Officer, responsible for administering contracts after they've been awarded. (Often one officer will make awards, and another C.O. will administer the contract, for the reason that the two activities require specialized personnel for each phase.) One of your contracts (you have some 400) is for a large radar antenna, being procured from a large midwestern producer. The contract was awarded on a negotiated basis; there was one other competitor, and these two were solicited because they are the only ones known to have the capability required, and subsequent negotiations resulted in the award to the midwestern firm.

The Government urgently needs the radars; you're aware that the awarding C.O. was under considerable pressure to get the proposals, negotiate, and place the contract as soon as possible. There haven't been any particular problems on the program, and development work is proceeding on schedule.

It is now some six months after the award.

One day your Contract Administrator on this program, Lou Ricardo, comes to you with a letter he has just received from the radar company's Contract Administrator. The letter says, "Now that we're about to deliver the prototype, how do you want us to bill you for running spares?" Running spares are the spare tubes and other parts that "run" with the antenna, and are for immediate maintenance requirements. Lou has looked over the original request for proposal (RFP), which clearly calls for the competitors to quote a price on running spares. It looks as though the company is trying to bill the Government *twice* for the same item, at an excess cost of almost a half million dollars.

You set up an appointment to meet the contractor's representatives the next day at his plant. Then you review in detail the pertinent materials in Lou's files, in preparation for the meeting. That afternoon you, Lou and Bob Satterwhite, your Administrative Chief, review the situation and conduct a role-playing session. You and Lou take opposing roles, to determine the relative strengths and weaknesses in the company's and the Government's positions. It looks as though you have an airtight case.

At the company's plant the next day, the representatives are cordial and seem sincere when they raise the question directly: "How do you want us to bill you—what contractual

coverage do you want in order to get the running spares?"
They're coming right out, waving a red cape in your eyes,
asking for another five hundred thousand bucks, when it's already in the contract!

You know that you can require them to deliver the
radar itself while the dispute about spares is going on, but the
set needs these spares for prototype testing. You're not about
to pay twice for the spares, however. What do you do?

*Tell the contractor to deliver the radar; and deliver the
spares, which you've already contracted for—see* 10, *page 109.*
*Tell the contractor to deliver the radar; and investigate
why he claims additional funds for the spares—see* 11, *below.*

11   You decided to tell the company to deliver the radar,
and then begin to probe his request for contract coverage and
the additional half million dollars for spares.

What unfolds is an eye opener.

After inquiring indirectly how he figured his costs, in
an effort to show that he had already covered the cost of the
spares, it develops that the agency had requested quotes on
some thirty-three line-items, prior to making the award. And
in response, the company had replied on *thirty-two* of these
items. Spares had *not* in fact, been included in his proposal
price. There was no intent on the part of the company to pull a
fast one. It just hadn't estimated what the spares' cost would be.

In making the crash-action award, the purchasing agent
and awarding Contracting Officer had not noticed this, and
had accepted the company's proposal as stated. Thus, the spares
had not been included in the contract price. You have no real
choice but to process an amendment covering the spares.

You find that things aren't always what they seem. The Government does sometimes make mistakes, although its record is very good. And you learn that contractors are not the money-gougers they're often portrayed to be. In fact, they're as interested in producing a quality product, on time, and within budget, as the Government is. Moral: the integrity of contractors is generally very high, even though first impressions may indicate otherwise.

Now go to the fourth decision.

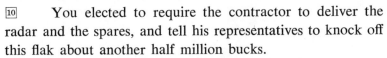

10   You elected to require the contractor to deliver the radar and the spares, and tell his representatives to knock off this flak about another half million bucks.

There's a problem here though, and you haven't gotten to the bottom of it. For one thing, you haven't found out his side of the story. For another, acting in a high-handed way might turn him off—not officially, but personally. His people are individuals too, like yours, trying to do a good job in turning out a quality product. You can castigate them and question their integrity, but it's likely to cost something in necessary teamwork and communications. And, just possibly, you might be wrong in your conclusion about his charging twice for the spares.

FOURTH DECISION

Here's a final case.

The contractor, located in New York, has completed a complex communications terminal and has done a good job. He delivered on schedule and managed the work to the extent that he made a reasonable profit on the fixed-price contract.

A pricing specialist learns, however, that one of the prime's subcontractors, located in Maryland, apparently made a *30 percent profit* on the components which he supplied to the prime. He has informal evidence to back this up.

Here's the problem facing you: your contract is with the prime, and you could, therefore, elect to close your eyes to the sub's profit. On the other hand, the best interests of the Government indicate that if the sub made an excess profit (15 percent is normally absolute tops), you should do something about it. The prime, however, wants no part in acting as middleman between you and the Maryland subcontractor regarding the sub's profit.

What do you do?

Withhold some of the prime's payment until you get cooperation from him and the sub—see 12, *below.*

Forget about the matter—see 13, *page 111.*

Try to get the sub to "volunteer" data on his profit— see 14, *page 111.*

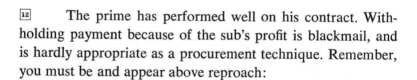

12   The prime has performed well on his contract. Withholding payment because of the sub's profit is blackmail, and is hardly appropriate as a procurement technique. Remember, you must be and appear above reproach:

> The necessity for maintenance of the highest standards of conduct by personnel engaged in procurement and related activities is a continuing one. Constant vigilance is required on the part of each individual to safeguard the reputation of (the Service) for honesty, courtesy, and fair dealing in its relations with contractors. Integrity and straightfor-

wardness in conduct is a way of official life, as much to be desired as in private life.

Now see 14, *below.*

18   You elected to forget about the sub's profit. After all, Chapter 6, "Rules of the Game," says, "The subcontractor's legal relationship regarding his rights and duties is with the prime, not with the Government. If the Government were to begin acquiring the massive data inherent in subcontracting, it could find itself in the extremely awkward, as well as very expensive, position of relieving the prime *de facto* of his responsibilities. Overcontrol already is a continuing problem."

But the best interests of the Government indicate that you should take some kind of action, and you can't pretend that you aren't aware of the sub's profit.

See 14, *below.*

14   You decided to try to get the sub to "volunteer" data on his profit, and this seems like a reasonable thing to do. You may not be able to require him to open his books to you, since your contract is with the prime rather than with the sub, and since the prime's price to the Government was fair and reasonable. But on the other hand, it's not in the best interests of the Government to do *nothing* about the sub's apparently excess profit.

Therefore you have your Contract Administrator draft a letter for your signature, asking the sub to provide information on his profit.

In a polite reply, he politely refuses.

You try again. Same result.

At this point, your practical alternative is to document the situation for record and future reference, and to live with it. You can also advise the Renegotiation Board, who will sheer off any excess profits the sub may have made (if the company has more than $1 million in defense business). But other than this, it's a matter of making a decision and recognizing the criticism that could come from hindsighters: "He *knew* they made an excess profit and failed to do anything about it!"

SKIN TOUGHENING

Your decisions are always subject to second-guessing, both at the time they're made and indefinitely into the future. Contracting develops a tough hide.

Even though he's in the thick of the fray, the Contracting Officer above all others must keep a cool, level head, be polite, and make decisions without letting his emotions cloud his judgment.

His protection lies in documenting every significant action he takes, because there's always a chance that this documentation may be needed to justify a past decision or procurement action. Government files are detailed, voluminous, and very expensive to maintain because of the possibility of criticism. But this documentation is necessary, as attacks on the procurement process and on specific procurements demonstrate.

DECISION-MAKING

The quickest way to go wrong in decision-making is to be concerned about what "they"—Review Board, your supervisor, unhappy bidders, columnists, congressmen, and hindsighters—will think if you make a particular decision. There's only one "group" whose interests the Contracting Officer needs to be concerned about: the best interests of the Government. Trying to save his own skin, or trying to please or appease vociferous individuals in either the Government or industry is certain to lead to erroneous decisions.

The Contracting Officer gets to feel after a while, "Okay, blast away, all you hindsighters; go ahead, and try to pick apart my decisions. I may make a mistake once in awhile, an error in judgment or in not having enough time to check everything to the extent I'd like. But I won't dodge my responsibilities, and you'll *never* pick me up on an error of intent." The C.O. feels, fiercely, that it's *his* money he's safeguarding. And it is, along with that of sixty million other taxpayers.

THE PRESSURES

The Contracting Officer isn't the only one who feels the strenuous pressures in contracting. In one contracts administration branch, where each of the thirty contract administrators had responsibility for more than a hundred contracts, half of these skilled individuals had a fatal or fatal-type illness over a two-year period.

Part of this pressure is due to time; part to not enough people to handle the increasing paper work; part to the volume of contracts; and part to crowded and noisy working conditions.

Contractors also feel the pressures caused by competition and tough negotiations. The vice-president of one major company, after an intense negotiating session which led to his company's winning an award, ended the pressure with a bullet.

DEALING WITH "ALUMNI"

The matter of how a Contracting Officer deals with former Government employees now in industry is so minor as to be negligible. Few of these alumni deal directly with the

Government, and rarely in a marketing capacity. The impression on a Contracting Officer in instances where an alumnus does contact him is a negative one. The C.O. is probably thinking, "This guy may have been in my shoes and now makes twice as much as I do (probably an overestimate), but he dang sure isn't going to gain any ground because of what he used to be." If there is a problem, and there probably isn't, it's how to avoid keeping the former Government employee's company from starting a little *behind* the starting line in a competitive situation. Most alumni know this, and know that it's smart *not* to display old school ties.

HALF-TIME SUMMARY

"The Government" doesn't negotiate and administer contracts. These functions are the responsibility of designated Contracting Officers and their representatives. The C.O. is right at the focal point where the Government gets its equipment or services and the contractor gets his money, where the best interests of the Government meet the profit motive of industry.

Contracting is a pressure-packed job, exciting but loaded with potential pitfalls and occasional abuse. In the words of Dodge City's most famous marshal, "It's a risky job; and it makes a man careful . . . and a little lonely."

9
The Game:
Second Half

On the other side of the procurement activity, the industrial half, the decision-making process is no less lonely, the pressures on individuals no less intense, the glare of publicity no less stark than on the Government side.

In providing the equipment and services required by the Services, a contractor strives to produce the item on time, to specifications, and within the contemplated cost. But there are broader matters that also concern him: what business to try to get? How to go about it? How to manage the work and overcome problems if the company *does* win a contract? How to plan for the facilities and plant required, how to retain or get the personnel needed, how to make a profit, in view of the accordion-like changes in defense work?

Someone has to come up with answers to these questions, and the answers don't come easily.

On specific programs, the project manager is the individual who determines whether the company makes or loses money, whether the Government winds up with a cost overrun or an underrun. The project manager is responsible for meeting cost, schedule and performance objectives. We'll take a look at what he does in the next two chapters. But before he arrives on the scene, some far-reaching business decisions must be made.

WHAT BUSINESS SHOULD WE BE IN?

In any industry most companies are opportunists, and the defense industry is no exception. Opportunistic companies evaluate business opportunities, compare them with their own capabilities, and strive for profit based on these two factors.

The opportunists overlook a fundamental element: objectives. Over a period of years, the companies who set objectives and operate by plan, like the Littons and the Lockheeds, generally outstrip their opportunist competitors. Many companies however, including some that are very large, fail to define what business they want to be in, and the extent of their involvement.

Here's the effect in one company of not having well-defined objectives.

A medium-size defense producer, located in the middle-Atlantic states, had great technical ability in its field, and its products and services had an excellent reputation. But the company had never defined what business it should be in: whether components, systems or subsystems; whether air, space, ground, marine or submarine environment; whether development, primarily, or production. Consequently its marketing troops went off in many directions, looking for business they, *as individuals,* thought their company wanted. And they brought back business opportunities, sometimes after months of traveling and marketing effort.

These opportunities were usually presented to a company committee, which determined whether or not to submit proposals. This generally occurred shortly before the Government issued a request for proposals. *Not until this point* did the company give any real thought to the business it wanted.

In one instance, a marketing representative spent more than half a year tracking a forthcoming program for which the Air Force's Electronic Systems Division was about to request proposals. The committee then decided that no, the company didn't want that particular kind of business. In another situation the committee gave a lukewarm go-ahead to submit a proposal for production of components; but the company's engineers effectively ambushed the marketing effort by submitting a grossly overweight, overcost, underperformance response because the work wasn't challenging enough.

Not all the business opportunities went before the committee. Some just happened. In one case, the company committed itself to developing a product line and, using its own funds, rounded up the technical talent needed and set to work. But the company found out a year later that it was in an extremely competitive field, and worse, that its technology was well behind that of its competitors.

In another major effort, the company developed a product line that seemed to have great promise because of its adaptability to individual customers' requirements. Again it used its own funds. But just after it began marketing the concept, the company discovered the line would compete with the parent company's commercial products. Two years' development, two million dollars, the product's cute

little trade name, and huge quantities of morale went
down the drain when the parent said, "You not only
don't market it, but you *forget that it ever existed*—
understand?"

The cost of not defining business objectives is tremendous, in time, money, and talent. If this company had defined
its market *before,* rather than *after* opportunities arose, it would
have added at least 20 percent to the effectiveness of every one
of its employees. In effect, this would have added 2000 employees, at no added cost.

Clear objectives are absolutely essential to planning and
to operations. After all, how can a company or an individual
go from where he is now to where he wants to be, if he doesn't
know where he wants to be?

WHAT CAPABILITIES SHOULD WE HAVE?

The capabilities a defense contractor has today—its technical talent, financial capabilities, the type and extent of test
and production facilities—aren't necessarily those it will need
tomorrow. In no other industry do these factors change so
rapidly as in aerospace, where both volume and technology are
a constantly changing kaleidoscope.

A company might enlarge its production facilities for
today's requirements only to discover that tomorrow the facility
is idle. It may find that it doesn't have either the special skills
or the number of scientists and engineers required to compete
on a forthcoming development program. Or it may learn that
raising money for operations or for expansion is a major problem because its earnings record is just so-so.

Comparing its present capabilities with those it will need in the future—and taking action accordingly—develops a tough, practical, flexible planner in the defense industry. On a clear day the planner can see for maybe two or three years; but his crystal ball is rarely crystal clear. In the forest-products industry, by contrast, leading companies plan fifty to one hundred years into the future.

One of the problems always present is, "What if we overcommit our facilities?" In practice, a company must have more proposals in the mill than it has capabilities of handling, because it will win on only a fraction of these proposals. But what if it bats better than its historical average? Or, worse, what if it hits *lower* than it has in the past; what if its facilities are under-committed?

This is the kind of thing that makes subs and primes. If a company does well on prime awards, it subcontracts the overflow to others. If it doesn't do so well, it looks for subcontracts. North American Rockwell's Los Angeles Division, which produced the F-86 and B-70, has become mainly a subcontractor in recent years.

BUSINESS OPPORTUNITIES

"What's available?" This is the "now" question.

The defense industry is a hungry industry. It wouldn't be cited for excessive optimism and buying-in if it weren't. The hunger pangs grew less intense when the burden of risk was shifted from Government to industry, in the mid-'60s, through increasing use of incentive contracting. But no company has assurance that its business under contract, and likely follow-on business, will sustain it in either the present or in the future.

Contract cancellations, stretch-outs, and cutbacks require a constant, intense effort to acquire new business.

A company's chart of likely defense sales looks like a bathtub: known and likely sales slope downward, maintain a low level, and then pick up as proposal efforts begin to yield future revenue. Filling in the bathtub is the job of the marketeers. The way they do it is by ferreting out business opportunities, getting a good understanding of an Armed Service's problem (i.e., why it needs a particular strategic or tactical system, for instance), and preparing the people back at the company for the request for proposal. If marketing and the proposal team do their job well, the company should submit enough winning proposals to fill in the tub.

But proposals are expensive to prepare; a major proposal effort can cost a million dollars or more ($50 million in the final F-15 competition). Therefore a company needs to rifle, rather than shotgun, the business opportunities, concentrating on those where it has the best chance of winning. (The company of the undefined objectives was an example of the shotgun approach.) The decision to submit a proposal is not one to take lightly, and a proposal must be well prepared. A poor one is worse than none at all.

Because of the importance of proposals, it's worth taking a brief look at how they come into being.

THE PROPOSAL

The proposal, in the defense business, is the point of sale. Its purpose is to show the Government customer that the company has the capabilities, understanding of the problem, approach to a solution, and experience to do the job.

The key to a winning proposal is a good grasp of the customer's problem. ("The customer" is not one all-embracing Government or Department of Defense; it is a number of major agencies and procurement centers, each of which is a potential customer.) This means learning as much as possible about the customer's requirements before the RFP is issued. A company that has not invested considerable marketing and engineering time *before* the RFP comes out shouldn't submit a proposal; it has already lost.

TEAMING

If a company makes a tentative decision to submit a proposal, it casts about for a dancing partner: who (in the case of a prime) are the subcontractors who will contribute the most to a winning proposal? In the case of a sub the question is who is most likely to get the prime contract award?

It is not easy to select a winning partner. One contractor elected not to team up with North American Aviation on the Apollo program because it thought North American's chances of winning were slight. North American not only won, but it has been for years the number one NASA contractor—by a wide margin—because of the Apollo program.

THE TIME ELEMENT

Usually the Government procurement agency allows thirty to sixty days for preparing proposals, and this is always less than companies would like to have for responding. But if they had 150 days, it still wouldn't be "enough." Restricting the time helps reduce companies' costs of proposal preparation, and reduces the administrative lead time in placing a contract.

The effect of having too little time is that preparing proposals is the most hectic, intensive, grinding activity in a hectic, intensive, grinding industry. A company that is trained and organized to react within the short time allowed has a marked advantage over competitors who are not so prepared.

ORGANIZING THE PROPOSAL EFFORT

The first action taken by a company when it receives the request for proposal is the bid/no bid decision. In practice, this decision should have been made long before receiving the RFP, subject to a quick review of the proposal request to determine whether there are any surprises in it. If marketing has provided the required intelligence, there should be no major surprises.

A proposal manager would previously have been selected, usually a well-qualified individual with a technical background and substantial experience in management. Often he will become the project manager if the company wins the proposal competition.

The job of managing the proposal effort is a small project management job in itself: producing a high-quality product (the proposal), meeting the submittal deadline, and keeping within the budget allotted by the company for the proposal effort.

The team selected by the proposal manager usually includes a system engineer, design engineers, program planning and control specialists, a product-assurance specialist, production and support people, cost analysts, a contract administrator, and publications representatives and others as the need arises.

These people work together in a "bull pen," usually a large room where they can work without interruption for the twelve to sixteen hours a day required for the integrated effort. On a major proposal, the "room" may be an airplane hangar filled with two football fields' worth of desks, mock-ups, blackboards, files, and other impedimenta.

Toward the end of the proposal period, the engineers and the project manager will often roll out their sleeping bags and spend full time at the company. As might be expected, this sometimes is a critical strain on family life.

PROPOSAL CONTENT

What these people are working to produce, as the days tick by, is three documents.

☐ A technical proposal, which outlines the problem and the company's approach to solving it. (This may amount to two or more volumes, with additional volumes as appendices.)

☐ A management proposal, outlining the contemplated project organization, related experience, master plan and schedules, and approach to anticipated management problems.

☐ A cost proposal, with a breakdown of costs and supporting data, summary of the cost/schedule/performance control system to be used, funding summary, and estimating techniques used in computing the cost and price.

The purpose of these documents is to answer the customer's questions, "What are you proposing to do? How are you going to manage it? How much will it cost, and why?"

REVIEW, PUBLICATION AND DELIVERY

The cost proposal is developed toward the later stages of the effort, when the technical proposal begins to firm up. But determining costs isn't just a matter of adding together individual cost estimates; these estimates have to be scrutinized for realism, economic factors (e.g., inflation), "excess water," and for duplication of costs. The cost proposal also depends on marketing and management estimates as to what the contract is likely to "go for," how much the customer has budgeted for the program, and what the competitors are likely to bid.

Usually, compared to the market factors, the initial cost estimate is too high. But by this time there's a problem: there isn't enough time to ask each cost estimator for revisions. The only feasible way to get the cost figures in line is for someone with the necessary authority, a division or company manager, to spend the final Saturday and Sunday of the period chopping and slashing away at cost estimates in order to develop a competitive price. Later, if the company wins the competition, it faces the consequences: how to live within the contract price, which is even lower (as a result of negotiations) than the submitted price, which in turn may be 50 percent lower than the estimates submitted by the company's estimators. The situation is particularly sticky if the contract is a fixed-price one. Herein lies the birth of the project manager's cost problems.

Meanwhile, the technical publications people have been screaming for the engineers to release graphic and narrative information for the technical proposal. At the latest possible hour, great mounds of typewritten material, pen and pencil scratchings, sketches, and cost data descend on the publications group for printing and reproduction. For two or three days the publications people work around the clock getting this mass of material ready for delivery.

Finally, on the morning of the due date, the bundle of proposal material is dropped in the waiting arms of the marketing representative. He races for a plane and whirs off to deliver the proposal to the customer.

Meanwhile, back at the plant, the proposal manager, publications people, and others of the team slump, groggy-eyed, behind the wheels of their cars and head for home in the early-morning sun to reintroduce themselves to their families.

CONCLUSION

A company that successfully meshes its objectives, capabilities, and opportunities will win its share of proposals.

But the game has just begun to get interesting with submission of a proposal. If it wins, a company has the honor of hanging onto a tiger's tail for several years. (If it loses, there's no excitement at all.) Stepping into the role of Tiger Fighter comes the project manager, who will do battle with the monster.

10
Of Tigers and Tiger Fighters

On the outside, a defense plant looks about like any other plant. Inside, it's a cage full of tigers and tiger fighters. These are the projects it has captured and the project managers whose job is to dominate the beasts.

These man-eaters come in assorted shapes and sizes, but they all have three characteristics in common—claws and fangs that make the tiger fighter's job interesting:

☐ A schedule that's possible to meet, provided nothing unexpected happens (that is, if the tiger realizes that it must live by the clock).

☐ Tight cost constraints that the project or program manager (PM) had a remote possibility of meeting, prior to negotiations. (There's a possibility the starving monster won't make a snack of the tiger fighter.)

☐ Technical performance requirements (the plane has to fly so fast, with a certain load, etc.) that are so

advanced and complex that no one knows for sure
whether they can be met. (There are no particular
problems here, however, provided the tiger forgets
its hunger pangs and the tormenting alarm clock,
and also changes into a lamb.)

The tiger fighter, or project manager, has come a long
way in the past few years though, in terms of protective equipment. Now he's armed with a chair, a whip, and a stiletto.
(Pistols are not allowed, for fear of damaging the tiger.)

Considering these luxuries and controls, the project
manager in deepest aerospace now has a relatively plush, cushy
job. Old timers (a few survive) recall when the game didn't
have all that fancy gadgetry. They point to the PM's counterparts in commercial/industrial projects, like brands managers
and new products managers, who grapple with their monsters
barehanded: little authority, flexible performance requirements,
and none of this cumbersome cost-schedule-performance-
control regalia. And they recall how it was in the old days, when
it took *guts* to run a program, and let the schedule and costs
fall where they may.

THE REASON FOR TIGER FIGHTERS

Once there was a time, during World War II and Korea,
when arms were relatively simple and were needed in huge
quantities; the problem was production. (This was an era when
MIC was accorded the title Arsenal of Democracy.) A Contract
Administrator, in industry and in the Government, kept an eye
on how the contract was going and saw to delivery schedules
and costs.

But things changed during the '50s. Weaponry and support systems (like command and control systems, and ground
support systems) became complex, and the premium was not

so much on production as on development. In addition to this complexity, weapons came to be looked upon as *systems,* rather than individual pieces of hardware. For instance, a missile system included the bird itself, real estate for the launching site, provisions for maintenance and spare parts, training the operating and maintenance personnel, preparing manuals and documentation, and so forth. As a result, many more functions had to be coordinated than a Contracts Administrator was capable of: systems analysis, system engineering, detailed engineering, fabrication, assembly, subsystem testing, system testing; and a lot of support activities: logistics support, training, publications; and always there were tight specifications and inspections. In addition, changes and changes to changes flowed like a never-ending stream.

The Services and industry realized that with so many things happening, it would be easy for something, like time, money or performance, to get lost in the shuffle. For this reason the Services, particularly the Air Force, established a job where one individual would be responsible for everything that happened on a project. He became the focal point for seeing that nothing slipped through the cracks. Industry, too, recognized the need for a single responsible individual, and established project managers. Thus the job of tiger fighters was born.

There are differences between the tiger fighter and other management species. For instance:

☐ The tiger fighter's job, his particular tiger, has never been tamed before; it's unique, whereas other managerial jobs involve some degree of repetition.

☐ The tiger fighter is a sort of swoose—a combination businessman, engineer, controller, lawyer, and chaplain.

☐ The tiger fighter is working to complete his project as soon as possible, and when he does, his job is finished. The functional manager's job normally goes on indefinitely.

☐ The tiger fighter has no line authority over most of the people working on his project; they report to functional management. And therein lies his basic problem.

☐ Dealing as he does with a sizable number of organizations and individuals in various Government agencies and industrial companies, the tiger fighter must ensure that communications are clear and prompt, and that everyone understands the project's objectives. "Communicate" is not a buzz word; it's an absolute necessity.

Probably everyone has heard about the two masons. One, when asked what he was doing, replied that he was laying bricks. The second answered, with no small amount of pride, "*I'm* building a cathedral!" It's not generally known, but the second man was summarily fired. He should have been building a garage. Getting "the word" is vital on a project.

CHARGE!

As soon as the tiger bounds through the front door, there's great temptation for the project team to charge right into it and show it who's boss. We'll dominate you, you murderous, beady-eyed beast! You don't have the *guts* to come out of that corner and fight!

After the tiger has devoured a few assistant tamers and the project has incurred substantial costs with no visible signs of progress, the need for a battle plan becomes apparent. Without a plan, in fact, the tiger is sure to win.

Managing a project isn't like building houses, or making pills or Chevy II's, where each one is about like the last one. A housing contractor or a manufacturer *knows* how he is doing, because he's produced a bunch of them before. He knows (or should know) whether he's on schedule, within budgeted costs, and how his product will perform. On a defense project, the yardstick for measuring status can't be a comparison of current versus previous projects, because there *aren't* any similar previous projects. The standard for knowing "how we're doing" has to be a comparison of "actuals" (actual costs, progress, technical achievement) versus the *plan* for the current project. A clear, comprehensive plan is an absolute necessity.

Stripped to its essentials, project management is setting objectives and taking action where action is needed. But how does the PM know where action is needed? Some PM's go by seat of the pants intuition; and they get mauled. Knowing where action is needed is a matter of knowing where the project actually stands, and comparing this to where it should stand. The first place to take action is where actuals are most out of line compared to the plan. The PM who operates this way may also get mauled, but he will at least get in some good licks of his own.

The framework for the project plan is a breakdown of what the deliverable items consist of (e.g., wings, fuselage, engines, landing gear, electronics, etc.) down to small assemblies. Each of these levels of hardware is assigned a target date and target cost, as well as performance requirements. This is called the work breakdown structure, or WBS.

Each part of the work is assigned to either a subcontractor on a contractual basis, or to an in-house department of the prime's own organization. In-house work is usually covered by a Work Authorization from the project office, which cites what is to be done, the time limits, and manpower and cost limitations. The Work Authorization doesn't have the teeth of a contractual arrangement, of course, but it is nevertheless a documented basis for going ahead with project tasks.

Without a *Work Authorization,* the tiger fighter is paying for open-end effort, rather than achievement.

Without a *work breakdown structure,* the tiger fighter may try to control project operations through the company's functional organization structure; and he may never realize that this is a major reason for his losing control.

Without a *plan,* the PM knows only where he is and where he wants to go; he doesn't know how he's going to get there. And without a plan for keeping people informed, he may wind up building a garage instead of a cathedral, or vice-versa.

THE PROJECT ORGANIZATION

With a few rare exceptions, the project manager/tiger fighter doesn't have a fully projectized organization, one which reports solely to himself. Most of the people working on his project report to other managers. The reason for this is that engineering talent and production facilities, for instance, are required on more than just one project; and because of the limited duration and hazardous existence of defense projects, no company can afford to give a PM exclusive use of all the resources he needs.

These factors gave rise to the "matrix-type organization," so named because the project organization cuts across the vertical functional organizations, as in Figure 1.

The project manager has a relatively small number of key people who report to him, including project control personnel and systems people (system analysts, system engineers,

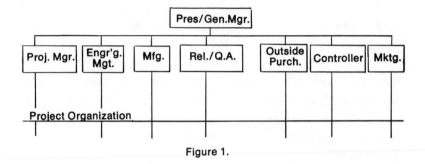

Figure 1.

and system test people, for instance). But he depends on people in other areas for detailed engineering, manufacturing, purchasing and subcontracting, controller support, and so on.

Actually a company has a number of tigers and tiger fighters within its confines, and the matrix looks like this:

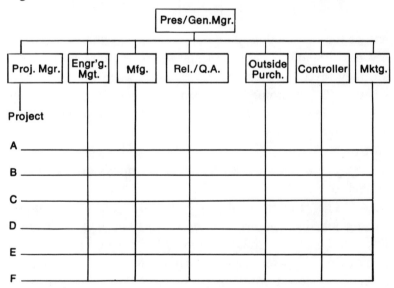

Figure 2.

The project managers typically report to a director or vice-president or, depending on the criticality of the project, to the general manager.

Granted that there are advantages of a matrix organization over either a fully projectized or fully functionalized arrangement, the foremost problem facing the project manager is how to get the greatest possible effort and devotion to his project from people over whom he has no direct authority. The intersection of the engineering organization for instance and the project organization is like the intersection of two streets,

and at the intersection there are engineers wondering, "Who's my boss? Should I look to Engineering for direction? After all, they say when I can go on vacation, when I'll get a raise, whether I'll get promoted. Or, since I'm spending most of my time working on Project A, is he the guy who's my boss? And what authority do I have over the guy who's subcontracting part of my work?"

These same questions are in the minds of individuals at each one of the intersections.

The solution to this problem is not the simple one of writing job descriptions. It's the more basic one of defining responsibilities and relationships. Many tiger-fighting companies (in both defense and nondefense industries) haven't yet successfully coped with this problem. A large Western electronics company, for example, had two conflicting directives on responsibility for subcontracts. One directive said that the project engineer is responsible for all work (in-house and sub-contract) assigned to him; the other said that subcontracts are the sole responsibility of the subcontracts administrator. In effect, the engineer and subcontract administrator were told, "Here, you two figure out who's supposed to do what." The loser in this situation is the project manager.

Here in microcosm is a typical problem and solution:

Problem: An engineer on Project A is going to sub-contract part of his work. It's clear that the engineer has responsibility for technical direction of the subcontracted portion, and that the subcontracts administrator is responsible for negotiating and administering the contract. But some aspects aren't so clear. Who has responsibility for cost control? For schedule control? For integrating cost/schedule/performance controls? And where does the project manager fit in the subcontract picture?

One *solution* is to define clearly who does what, and to document this arrangement. (Otherwise, the assistants to the tiger fighter may wind up fighting each other instead of the tiger.)

> P—Who has *primary* responsibility—i.e., who has the ball for the job?
>
> I—Who should get *information* on actions taken?
>
> C—Whom should *coordination* be effected with, before action is taken?
>
> A—Who has approval authority, where higher-level approval is required?

A "PICA" chart helps define the relation of the engineer, subcontracts administrator and the project manager, as in Figure 4.

"Who": / —"What"—	Subcontracting	Engineering Direction	Cost & Budget	Schedule & Progress
Engineer	C	P	I	C
Subcon. Administrator	P	I	P	P
Project Manager	I	C	A	C

Figure 4.

The chart clearly shows that the subcontracts administrator has primary responsibility for cost and budget control; but that he must get the project manager's approval for changes, and that he must provide information on planned and actual expenditures to the engineer.

A chart of this type can cover the whole project organization on one piece of paper, and it goes a long way toward reducing frictions and individual decisions. But more than that, it ensures that responsibilities are covered.

CONTROLLING THE MONSTER

The tiger fighter normally holds a weekly review of costs and progress status, and meets at least weekly (and informally on a continuing basis) with technical personnel on technical problems. In addition, he has an opportunity to show his cuts and bruises at least once a month to company management, and he keeps the customer posted by monthly written reports and periodic in-person reviews.

His struggle with the tiger is observed by many.

Occasionally in the past, a tiger fighter has shielded company management and the customer from knowing the truth about a project's problems. Eventually the lid would blow off, sometimes taking his head with it.

Many control techniques have been tried on Government projects; some have proved to be Rube Goldberg contraptions, and others are highly effective. Some of both types are glanced at in Chapter 11.

In controlling his monster, the project manager has several types of authority, including higher management backing and stated authority. But when the going gets tough, as it inevitably does, he has only one real weapon: control of the funds. Without this whip, the PM is just a C-ration in tiger fighter's clothing.

THE CHANGING BEAST

The tiger that charged into the contractor's plant isn't the same one that ultimately gets tamed. It changes. In the process of analyzing and solving technological problems, opportunities come up for improving the product and its capabilities. Some of these are approved as changes in scope. The effect is that these benefits are available to the using Service when the item becomes operational.

These changes result in a somewhat different item from what was initially contracted for, and have to be paid for under modifications to the contract. This effect is almost always referred to as a cost *overrun* when actually it is a cost *growth;* the difference is the cause, whether by lack of intent (overrun) or by direction (growth).

Sometimes the changes come thick and fast, as they did on the early long-range missiles. Any one change may go through a number of steps before it is approved, and the flow of hundreds of these changes requires a control system. As a result, configuration management came into being, whereby the Service (Air Force) and the contractor would have records and could know what the innards of a Titan or Minuteman, for instance, looked like.

THE FUNDING GAMBLE

The Government's fiscal year and funding habits present an interesting problem to the tiger fighter and his company. The problem is the new year's funds may not be available for two or three months after the July 1 start of the new fiscal year; and what does the project manager do meanwhile? Should he let the tiger up for breath? If he does, can he later get it back under control? Should he ask the company to go ahead and fund the effort until the Government's funds come along? Should he stop work? Stretch it out? Pay volunteers with play money from his Monopoly game?

The Government, of course, hopes the company will go ahead, using its own funds. But the Contracting Officer can't make any promises, actual or implied, about whether the money will be coming through. If he were to say, "Sure, go ahead, do the work. After all, you've got to keep on schedule," he would be personally liable if the Government were later to cancel the program during this funding drought.

The PM usually goes hat in hand to his company's management and asks the company to support the program with its own money until the new fiscal year's funding catches up. Amazingly enough, most companies go along with this request. The company, too, is interested in subduing the tiger.

If the company guesses wrong in taking the risk, it may lose many times whatever profit it might have made, and this has sometimes happened. If it guesses right, the Government customer hardly even notices the risk assumed. The customer's attention is riveted on the tiger fighter, and how come he paused there for a moment in his struggle?

CONCLUSION

As system complexity and the performance of today's defense systems increase, fewer companies have the capability for taking on total project responsibility. One of the resources required is a high level of technological expertise, and others are proven production and financial capabilities.

But another resource required is tiger fighters who have the know-how, equipment, experience, and endurance to battle the tiger. These management capabilities are required not only in large companies; subcontractors' tigers are often as tough to subdue as prime ones.

To the tiger fighter, there comes a time when he thinks there *must* be an easier way to earn a living. Maybe he should have paid closer attention in high school to that bit about The Lady or the Tiger. Maybe he should have stayed with the violin, or gone into the ministry as his mother said.

But there isn't much time for reminiscing when you're sailing around in a cage at the end of a tiger's tail.

11
Controlling the Monster

TOOLS OF THE
TIGER-FIGHTING TRADE

On an August day in Stockholm, Sweden in 1628, townspeople, government dignitaries and other high officials gathered at the ways of a Stockholm shipbuilding company, wearing their best clothes and in holiday spirit. This was the day the mighty warship Vasa was finally to be launched.

The Vasa was a beautiful ship, of the best oak and other materials, worthy of the pride all felt toward her. Its two gun decks bristled with sixty-four bronze cannon poking their muzzles through two levels of open gun ports. A lion on the bowsprit roared defiance. This was a vessel equal to any in the world.

When the speeches and traditional ceremonies were finally completed, workers removed the blocks and ties that held the ship in place, and this mightiest ship of the Navy began to slide down the ways. Picking up speed, it smacked into the water. The crowd cheered and waved to those on board, about

450 people, including the wives and children of some of the dignitaries and officers.

The ship's captain ordered the sails set to catch the light breeze. As the sails filled, the ship leaned farther and farther to its port side. Water began pouring in through the open ports on the lower gun deck; this made the ship heel still farther on its side. Then, a mile from its launching point, the ship sank from view. Most of those on the Vasa were saved, but this sudden turn of events ruined the whole day for others.

Candles on the drawing boards burned late that night.

Work on the Vasa had started three years earlier, and we can be pretty certain that the launching was several months or more behind schedule, and final costs were considerably more than originally expected. The cost overrun and schedule slippage might have been forgiven, however, if the ship had met its performance requirements. It probably did meet most of these requirements—firepower, cruising range and speed, for instance; it's just that no one expected the ship would turn out to be a submersible.

We can picture an earlier-day member of Sweden's Upper House rising to say to his colleagues, "The absence of effective controls over the procurement of weapons systems and the existence of questionable practices in the Department of Defense is creating economic inefficiencies and waste, a subsidy to defense contractors, and an inflated defense budget.

"Huge cost overruns, waste, and inefficiency have become the hallmarks of military procurement . . . and far-reaching changes must be brought about in order to obtain economy of operations in the Department of Defense. . . ."

Three hundred and thirty years after the Vasa disappeared, a diver discovered a "wall of wood" at the bottom of Stockholm harbor. Clambering up the side, he saw two levels of open gun ports: it had to be the Vasa. In 1961 the warship was raised and hauled to shore to become a museum.

TECHNICAL PERFORMANCE

Everyone assumes that the ship will float, the plane will hit mach three or four, the man will bring back samples from the moon. In an era when spectacular technical accomplishments are almost taken for granted, the glare of publicity shines harshly on time and money: why did it cost so much, and take so long?

Nevertheless, the degree to which a chunk of hardware performs is of first importance. If the Vasa had cost only $80,000 instead of the expected $90,000, and even if it had been launched ahead of schedule, these savings in time and money would have gone down the drain along with the ship itself. Failures in technical performance (as distinct from management performance) would have nullified this excellence in management.

In modern-day armaments, America's Armed Services have concentrated first on performance, because lives depend on first-class hardware. In response to the Services' requirements, industry has produced a staggering list of list of high-performance equipment, including vehicles and support systems for space exploration. (High praise for U.S. management comes from a leading Soviet physicist, seventy-five-year-old Pyotr L. Kapitsa, who acknowledges that better science management techniques may have enabled the U.S. to beat the Soviet Union to a manned lunar landing. He also said there was no "lack of funds" for space exploration in his country. *(Aviation Week and Space Technology,* 13 October 1969, p. 15.)

Every project has technical performance objectives unique to itself, whether the product is a ship, a main battle tank, an electronic intelligence system or an office building. Software, too, such as a computer program or the final report of a study project, has standards of performance that must be met.

One of the difficulties with technical performance is how to measure it during the course of a project. Partly, this difficulty is due to the problem of determining whether progress achieved is in line with what the final performance must be (e.g., knowing, during design and construction, that the Vasa wouldn't list excessively), and partly the difficulty is due to the fact that technical performance can't be quantified by any one measurement, as can time and money. Weight, size, shape, reliability, maintainability, and all kinds of performance criteria are factors in describing technical performance.

The difficulties in measuring technical performance carry over in trying to evaluate technical achievement against money spent and progress achieved. The problem is how to know, before the project is completed and it's too late to do anything about it, whether technical performance, money spent and time consumed are in line with each other. So far no one has a solid handle on integrating all three factors.

THE SIGNIFICANCE OF TIME

A project, by definition, has definite starting and completion dates, and the penalties for not completing the project on time are both immediate and long range. The immediate penalty is higher costs. Almost invariably when a project stretches out, it uses more labor, more overhead, and invites more changes, all of which cause a growth in costs. The longer-range penalty of a stretch-out, the shortened useful life of an item, costs even more, in both dollars and unpreparedness.

THE CRITICAL PATH

    For centuries, project scheduling consisted of making a list of things that had to be done, with their start and completion times. Then, during World War I, there occurred a real breakthrough when Henry L. Gantt, a management consultant working for the Government, developed the Gantt or bar chart. Gantt's scheduling method gives a picture of time, and looks like this:

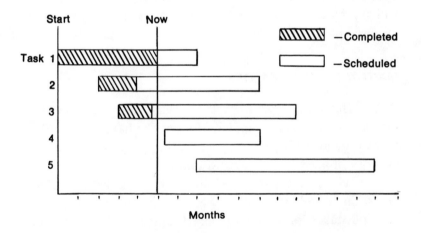

Figure 1.

    Because a bar chart shows so clearly what's happening, it is still used on even the most complex programs as a summary of actual progress and scheduled progress.

But when programs began to be more complex, it was recognized that the bar chart had limitations. For instance, it didn't show the relationship between activities—what had to happen first before something else could be done. And it didn't go into the depth of detail required. An Apollo might have 50,000 events in development of the ground support equipment alone—far too many to show on a bar chart.

In answer to this problem, the Services and industry developed "critical path scheduling" in the late 1950s. By whatever name it takes—PERT (program evaluation and review technique), CPM (critical path method), CPM to a time scale, etc.—this scheduling method takes a network of interrelated activities and shows where the critical path lies. This is the path on which, if anything slips, the completion date will slip by a corresponding amount. A computer is necessary on large programs to figure where the critical path is.

MARTINIS AND POTATOES

But critical path scheduling isn't necessarily so complex as to require a computer. Housewives have used PERT/ CPM principles for years, every time they get a dinner ready. A network of activities for a roast dinner looks like Figure 2.

The critical path here is along the lines "heat oven" and "roast in oven." It's critical because if either of these two activities takes longer than planned, dinner will be that much later than scheduled. On the rest of the activities there's "slack" —time to spare—as long as she doesn't wait *too* long. If she's downing martinis while fixing the potatoes and the potatoes go in at 5 P.M., they (potatoes or martinis) will be served with dessert.

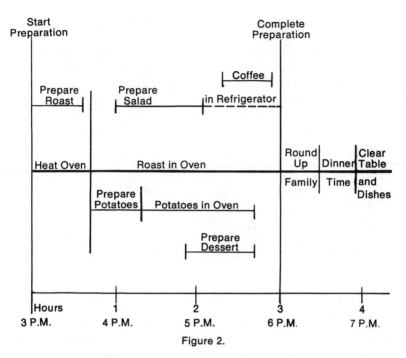

Figure 2.

For a bachelor, the critical path network is somewhat simpler:

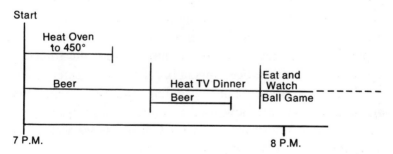

Figure 3.

The basic purposes of critical path scheduling are

☐ To see how to reduce the time from start to finish of a project. Project time can be reduced by knowing what's on the critical path, and then either doing things simultaneously (like rounding up the family while the roast finishes roasting) or doing them faster (like cooking the roast at a higher temperature).

☐ To see where slack is. This enables the cook to level her workload so that she doesn't alternately have so much time that martinis become a hazard, and then have too much to do at once, like an octopus. On a defense project, knowing where there's slack enables the tiger fighter to make the best use of his people, and to avoid overtime pay wherever possible.

If there's a time scale for reference, as in these diagrams, the cook can see when dinner will be ready, and can note the time to start salad, dessert, etc. On a defense program, having a calendar scale serves the same purpose.

Well, how good are PERT and CPM in practice?

They're pretty good. PERT is credited with having slashed *two years* off the Navy's development of the Polaris missile, and it has saved great amounts of time on other programs. (It could have been used by a well-known Genoese sea captain who was having trouble outfitting three ships for a voyage to the unknown. See Appendix III for The Enterprise of the Indies.) Critical path scheduling and other computer-oriented controls are now used in nondefense projects (construction and industrial/commercial projects) as well as on every major development project for defense. The Services and defense industry strive continuously to develop more advanced management aids for better visibility in project control.

THE EFFORT TO CONTROL COSTS

On one of the Surveyor landings on the moon, the head of Cal Tech's Jet Propulsion Laboratories (JPL) was asked to explain in laymen's terms how commands were given to the spacecraft. He replied, "We don't really *command* it to do anything; we send it *requests* to perform certain tasks."

In the same way, a project manager doesn't so much control costs as he makes valiant attempts at controlling costs. Even after deducting the effects of inflation and changes in scope, the record of overruns attests to the difference between "control" and "attempts."

PROJECT COST CONTROLS

The attempt to control project costs starts with the work breakdown structure (WBS): how much should each of the project elements cost? When this is established, a plan of expenditures (how much per week, for instance) is figured for each element. Effective cost planning considers how many dollars it will take to reach the various progress milestones for each item; this ties expenditures to the schedule, and the project manager (in Government and in industry) can figure whether progress is what it should be for the money spent.

This plan of expenditures, or budget, is figured on a dollar basis and often also on a manpower basis, since manpower is normally the largest single item of expense.

Controlling costs on a defense project is like that of any other project, in most ways: it's a matter of comparing actual costs against planned costs, and taking action to reduce expenditures where they are getting higher than they should be. Cost controls involve practical problems, such as getting cost reports in sufficient time to *do* something where costs are too high; checking to make sure no one is "loading" the contract (making charges against it when these costs should have been charged to some other project); and foreseeing trouble spots and their effect on cost control and fiscal control.

And there's an inherent problem with a project budget: how accurate can a budget be for a tiger that has never been tamed before?

But the main problem comes in relating expenditures to progress, and there have been some massive attempts to relate the two. This is the matter of integrated controls, which we'll look at a little further in this chapter.

LARRY MILES' IDEA

Larry D. Miles was a purchasing agent in General Electric's headquarters when he was asked in 1948 to explore the problem of value analysis. This assignment came about as a result of the company's vice-president for purchasing having noticed, during World War II, that when substitute materials were used, many of these substitutions resulted not only in lower cost but also in an improved product. "It happened so often by accident that we decided to try to make it happen on purpose," he said.

Miles' objective was to determine analytical methods that could be developed to reduce costs of purchased subassemblies through changes in design or specifications. His background in mechanical engineering was important in analyzing a product's purpose or function and determining whether the same function could be accomplished by eliminating parts, by using less expensive ones, or by using parts of a simpler design. In one of his first analyses, Miles demonstrated that a part costing $67.50 per thousand could be replaced by one that cost about $3.82 per thousand.

In 1949 the boom in television sets posed a problem: how to produce the volume of television tubes required, and how to reduce the cost, which was excessive due to rejects, problems in handling, and other causes. Applying value-analysis techniques to the process of putting the glass picture tube together with the electronic circuitry, Miles' value-analysis division discovered they could show the glass supplier how to reduce his unit prices by one-half, with further savings of 40 percent in GE's process for sealing in the electronic components. Value analysis began to spread to other manufacturers.

But value analysis was used primarily on parts already produced. Then the question popped up, why not engineer value into products *before* they are released for production?

This gave birth to value engineering (VE).

The Department of Defense adopted VE wholeheartedly in the McNamara era, and the Secretary of Defense gave strong personal support to the program.

In most cases, the documented cost savings have been used to satisfy requirements that would otherwise have gone unfunded. Instances where real dollars are returned for reuse are not unusual, however. Loral Electronics returned a check for $418,000 to the Navy as a result of value engineering; the Naval Ordnance Plant in Louisville returned funds in the amount of $583,000 in another instance.

In addition to cost savings, other benefits are realized from value analysis/value engineering. The American Ordnance Association, selecting 193 projects at random from 2000 value engineering change proposals, found these additional benefits:

　　78 percent reduced lead time
　　37 percent weight reduction
　　82 percent improvement in producibility
　　33 percent improvement in performance
　　71 percent improvement in quality
　　63 percent improvement in reliability
　　64 percent improvement in maintainability

ALONG CAME INCENTIVES...

As noted earlier ("Rules of the Game"), another broad-scale cost reduction technique has been increased use of incentive contracts. These contracts (fixed price, fixed price-incentive, and cost plus incentive fee) in large measure transfer the burden of risk from the Government to industry, and at the same time provide incentive to effect economies and share in cost savings. A company that reduces costs through value engineering, for example, may earn as much as 75 percent of the savings, although usually the contractor and Government split fifty-fifty.

The result of early changes from CPFF contracts to incentive contracts were impressive. The Secretary of Defense announced these savings, largely as a result of incentive contracting and value engineering:

> 1963—$1 billion
> 1964—$2.5 billion
> 1965—$4.6 billion

Elimination of gold-plating (e.g., value engineering), risk contracting, and closing of excess military bases constituted a three-pronged attack on expenditures which helped produce a Defense posture in the sixties that was better geared for its purpose than at any time since 1776.

INTEGRATING TIME, COST, AND PERFORMANCE CONTROLS

To control costs on a project, it's not enough to know that costs are within budget. Costs may be within budget but still be excessive because progress lags to the extent that catching up will push costs above the budgeted amount. Or, conversely, costs may be above budget; but there isn't a cost problem if progress is ahead of schedule by a corresponding amount.

The problem is one of relating actual and expected *costs* to actual and expected *progress,* and to actual and expected *technical performance.*

Controlling technical performance is difficult in itself, as pointed out earlier in this chapter. The closest approach to integrating this factor with time and money is to tie technical milestones to schedule milestones. Controlling the monster then becomes primarily a matter of correlating costs and progress. DOD has mounted some massive efforts to do this.

One of these massive efforts was PERT/Cost (P/C). This was an attempt to provide the program manager with progress-for-the-money data, in order that he could know or predict what specific problems he had on his hands. Within DOD and industry, almost all programs people jumped aboard the P/C bandwagon, although many had misgivings as to whether the massive data, massive cost of the data (which chewed substantially into the Defense budget) and massive complexity of the concept were worth the limited visibility provided. Nevertheless PERT/Cost carried on for three or four years, until the house of cards proved to be a crashing failure (although it crashed silently). P/C bandwagon riders are hard to find these days, although PERT/Cost is not yet a dead issue.

Currently DOD has another concept in the mill, under the name "cost/schedule control systems criteria," or C/SCSC for short.

C/SCSC came about because of the deficiencies of PERT/Cost. In effect, DOD said in 1968, "Okay, industry; if you don't like PERT/Cost, then *you* tell *us* how you propose to manage a major program. If your system meets the cost/schedule criteria we require, we'll go along with your system."

This sounded fine, but it wasn't that simple. For one thing, deciphering what DOD meant, in its one-hundred-page guide on the subject, was (is) a perplexing job, even for professionals in the business. After more than a year of C/SCSC-ing, only one contractor's system was known to have received approval.

Another problem with cost/schedule control systems criteria, as in PERT/Cost, is the sheer mass and cost of data. "Make sure you've got plenty of data, contractor, and send us a bunch of the same," doesn't guarantee any better visibility than face-to-face contact between the PM and his people. In fact, these great blizzards of paper often cloud his visibility and reduce the time available to him for fighting fires.

Simplicity, recognized as a virtue in engineering, sports, art and military planning, seems to have eluded DOD as a virtue in project management systems.

By starting with a solution (mounds of data) instead of with analysis of the problem, DOD has sometimes initiated solutions that prove to be ineffective and more complex than the problem itself, which is how to be sure of getting progress for the money spent (industry's role has generally been one of implementing solutions proposed by the Defense Department). Nevertheless DOD is keenly aware of the problem and has made significant efforts to solve it. (Appendix IV outlines a simple way for the tiger fighter to determine the health of his project, and to see where to take action in order to control costs).

THE ECONOMICS OF RISK-TAKING

On almost any development project, the elapsed time from start of development through deployment can be compressed, using critical path scheduling. A schedule that looks like this

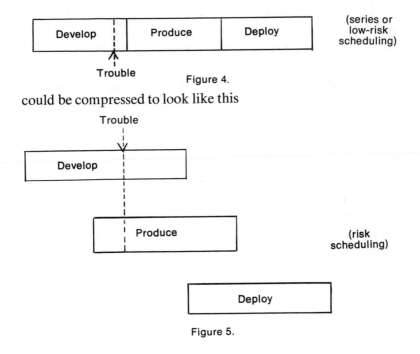

Figure 4.

could be compressed to look like this

Figure 5.

This, in fact, is what was done in the past on urgent requirements, such as the Atlas, because of our late start, and nuclear Polaris submarines.

Critics point out, however, "Sure you can save time, but look at the risk! Why, you're still designing and testing even when you're in production! What if you run into trouble half-way through development? You'll increase the costs of production and deployment by *millions*! Think of the waste!" And it's true; if trouble develops in *series* scheduling, it has little effect on production and deployment. But if the same trouble develops in *high-risk* scheduling, as it did on the main battle tank (MBT-70), it will result in expensive changes in production and deployment. For this reason a move to schedule development, production, and deployment on a low-risk basis is gathering momentum in DOD, due to Congressional pressures for economy.

But saving time is saving money, *even when the risks turn out the wrong way.* Here's why.

The Services used to produce hardware on a step-by-step basis. This is the way a B-29 or a B-36 was procured. A decade would pass before the item became operational, i.e., was in the hands of the users. In high-risk scheduling, e.g., Atlas missiles, the cost is greater due to redesign, reprocurement, etc.; but the same item can become operational in half the time.

Suppose development of a system begins in 1970, and the system will have a useful life until 1985, when advances in "competitors" technology will make it obsolete or obsolescent. If sure-thing scheduling is used—taking steps in series—and ten years go by before the system is operational, it will have a *five-year life* (1980-1985). With high-risk scheduling, on the other hand, the system could become operational in only five years, and would have a *ten-year life* (1975-1985).

Suppose now that with sure-thing scheduling the procurement cost is $1 billion. With only five years' useful life, the procurement cost is *$200 million per year.*

In comparison, high-risk scheduling might result in a procurement cost of $1.4 billion. But the system would have ten years' useful life as a result of the risks taken, and the procurement cost is *$140 million per year.*

In terms of *cost,* low-risk scheduling on a project saves money. In terms of *value,* however, low-risk scheduling is a very expensive way to go, in both dollars *and in gaps in preparedness.*

The fact that high-risk scheduling is more economical than sure-thing scheduling has been recognized for a long time in nondefense industries.

Many new products and processes have short commercial lives during which profits can be realized;
therefore several years wasted out of this period due
to dilatory research action may mean the loss of a
real profit opportunity.[1]
 Investment in new-product development is
an asset to those who had the foresight to start early
programs. It is an insidious threat to all others. Those
who are behind can't catch up easily . . . you would
have to cope with a built-in time lag of serious mag-
nitude. . . . The greatest rewards are going to those
who can tap and harness new technology.[2]

It would be perfectly logical, of course, to slow down
on military R&D if the competition would do the same. But our
intelligence isn't that good on their intentions and capabilities.
What we do know indicates they're taking just the opposite
course:

Crash programs are common in the (Soviet) strategic sector. Ustinov (Director of Soviet defense
industries Dmitri Fedorovich Ustinov) frequently
double-teams a project at least through the research
and development stage.[3]

And in production the competition doesn't seem to be dragging
its feet either:

Navy Nuclear Chief Hyman G. Rickover says the
Russians—determined never again to have to back
down as they did during the Cuban missile crisis—
rapidly are overtaking the U.S. submarine fleet. . . .
He said the Russians were expected to add 70 nuclear
submarines by 1974 compared to the United States'
26—including enough Polaris-type submarines to
match or surpass the United States' 41.[4]

Sometimes we forget, conveniently, that it takes a long time to build up the technology base required to produce advanced systems. A U.S.S.R. lunar probe took the first pictures of the far side of the moon in 1959. It wasn't until *six years later,* with an all-out effort leading to the Apollo landings, that the U.S. was finally able to duplicate this feat.

There's always the *chance,* of course, that if the U.S. pursues sure-thing scheduling, the U.S.S.R. and China will suddenly devote their weapons know-how to producing stereo consoles and striped toothpaste.

The problem in guessing wrong is that it's so hard to sit down if we lose something more personal than coin.

CONCLUSION

The mighty Vasa disappeared from view almost as soon as it was launched. Even though it came back into the world almost perfectly preserved, technology and the passage of time made a museum of what once was an advanced system of weaponry. The Queen Mary became a museum in one-tenth of the time.

Resting now on their charred bottoms are capsules of the Mercury and Gemini programs—relics of the space age, museum pieces in only one-tenth the time required for the Queen Mary.

Controlling projects is more than meeting cost, schedule, and performance objectives, important though these are. It's also recognizing that rewards go to those willing to take risks, and that time, not money, is the key factor in determining value.

12
Perspective

■ AMERICA'S WIDENING MILITARY MARGIN
Behind the disarmament talks lies the fact that technological competition with the U.S. is proving too much for the U.S.S.R. . . . What the Russians have been shooting for at disarmament conferences in London is quite clear. . . . They want to slow down the arms race, at least for a while, because the U.S. pace is too stiff for their existing technical resources to match. . . . The American strategic position, vis-à-vis Soviet Russia, is being steadily improved. . . . If ever it made sense for the U.S. to hold fast to the long-haul strategy . . . it certainly does now, when the U.S. power margin is widening. (Charles J. V. Murphy, "America's Widening Military Margin," *Fortune,* August 1957, p. 94.)

■ INTERNATIONAL OUTLOOK   The London arms control talks are nearing some kind of climax. Before the end of the month it should be clear whether the Russians mean to go on negotiating. . . . (*Business Week,* 3 August 1957.[1])

■ **INTERNATIONAL OUTLOOK**   Russian delegate
Valerian A. Zorin put the damper on the London dis-
armament talks this week. . . . (*Business Week,* 17
August 1957.[2])

■ **INTERNATIONAL OUTLOOK**   For all practical
purposes, Syria this week became a Soviet satellite.
. . . Washington is watching the Syrian situation with
foreboding. (*Business Week,* 24 August 1957.[3])

■ **BUSINESS ROUNDUP**   In a whirlwind farewell
performance as outgoing Secretary of Defense,
Charles E. Wilson made far-reaching economies in
defense spending involving cutbacks in missiles, the
mothballing of ships, the closing of training centers,
and trimming of maintenance costs. . . . ("Business
Roundup," *Fortune,* September 1957, p. 51.)

■ **RED MISSILE SHAKES PENTAGON**
- Russia's announcement of its intercontinental ballistic missile casts doubts on
  wisdom of defense cutbacks.
- The Pentagon insists that the Russians'
  success doesn't change the relative military power of the two countries.
- Critics, however, say that even the ballistic
  missile projects have been slowed down by
  budget cuts.

Over the past few months, the U.S. defense
program has been overhauled in an Administration
attempt to hold spiraling military expenditures down
to last year's level. Important aircraft and missile
projects have been cut back, canceled, and stretched
out.

This week's Russian announcement of a successful test firing of an intercontinental ballistic missile—beating the U.S. to the punch—puts these decisions in a new light. It is generating demands for a new review of defense policy . . . and has raised questions that perhaps over-all military spending should now be increased rather than reduced. . . .

• Sounding an Alarm—Critics like (Senator) Jackson take Russia's ICBM claim more seriously than the Administration seems to.

But there's not much Congress, on the verge of adjournment, can do to speed up the program. Indeed, Congress recently cut $400 million from funds requested for Air Force aircraft and missile production. . . .

• Latest Cuts—Even with the Soviet announcement, cutback announcements continued to flow from the Pentagon under the Administration's drive to bring fiscal 1958 Defense Dept. expenditures down to the $38 billion sum set in the initial military budget. . . . (*Business Week,* 31 August 1957.[4])

■ RUSSIA BALKS AT ARMS CONTROL   The London arms control talks finally fizzled out this week.. . . (*Business Week,* 7 September 1957.[5])

■ RUSSIA TAKES LEAD IN MISSILES   In the early dawn of October 5, somewhere east of the Ural Mountains, smoke enveloped the base of a monster rocket; the monster shook the ground with its thunder, climbed painfully into the air, and then shot skyward with a tail of flame. Something like 10 minutes later, the first artificial satellite—"Sputnik" to its Russian makers—was circling the earth.

● Meanings—In the long view of history, that event may well be remembered simply as a great human achievement, as the beginning of an era of exploration and maybe colonization out among the stars. But on the tense, heavily armed earth above which Sputnik circles, it has more immediate, more urgent, more ominous meanings.

First of all, it changed the world's picture of Russian technology and military strength. . . .

● Changed Issues—The new military balance has once more shifted the factors in the slow, complex negotiations aimed at easing the world's tensions. . . .

In Washington, the U.S. government began to re-examine its military policies. . . .

Key conclusion: Sputnik and its propulsion system, taken together, constitute a first-class intercontinental missile—plus trimmings. On its record, it should be capable of delivering a hydrogen warhead from its launching pad to any other spot on earth, and with considerable accuracy. It is definitely a more advanced missile than anything the United States has yet fired. It is almost certainly a more advanced weapon than this country's Atlas ICBM— which has had two unsuccessful tests to date—even after the bugs in the Atlas have been worked out. It is probably more advanced than the Titan, which is coming along behind the Atlas. . . . (*Business Week,* 12 October 1957.[6])

■ HOW TO REGAIN THE LEAD IN MISSILES   The Russians have demonstrated a clear lead on the United States in the long-range missile business. That is the ominous significance of the artificial satellite that began sweeping around the earth a week ago,

beeping steadily on the note of A-flat. And there is
no sense in kidding ourselves about it. . . . While we
are designing a propulsion system for a laboratory
device, the Russians have designed one capable of
handling a military weapon.

Moreover, there was no guesswork in the
firing of the Soviet rocket. It was set neatly in an opti-
mum orbit, and the Russians were able to announce
its orbit as soon as it was aloft. Clearly, they have an
accurate and reliable guidance system.

In the light of these two facts, it appears that
the Russians were telling the sober truth last summer
when they announced that they had perfected an
intercontinental ballistic missile. . . .

Obviously, we now need a crash program to
bring us even with the Russians in the science of
rocketry—and if possible to put us ahead of them.

Unless we are now willing to make whatever
effort is necessary to recapture the lead, we will
someday face an enemy so powerful that he can
dictate the terms of any co-existence he wishes to
permit us.

If the launching of the Soviet satellite spurs
us to make that effort, our humiliation will be worthwhile. For the steady beep-beep coming in from
space reminds us that a free society does not automatically produce a better technology than a regi-
mented system. That comforting theory holds true
only if a free society is willing to make voluntarily
some of the sacrifices a totalitarian state can command—and has commanded—of its citizens. (*Business
Week,* 12 October 1957.[7])

■ **WASHINGTON OUTLOOK**   Washington is upset,
frankly, by Russia's scientific gains.

There's more to it than the Red Sputnik—the Soviet satellite, launched well ahead of U.S. expectations. For perspective, you need to think back over the postwar years. Russia developed her first A-bomb much earlier than had been anticipated. The same was true of her first H-bomb. And, meantime, she flew new jet planes much earlier than had been expected. In the missile field, Red progress is way ahead of what our defense officials anticipated. Any doubt about Russia's claims of an intercontinental ballistic weapon disappeared when the little Red moon was put in the sky. . . .

The so-called lag in U.S. research and development will be investigated. The Democrats, with the next election contest for House and Senate control only a year away, will try to show that Eisenhower economies have hampered defense—permitted Russia to surge ahead in the arms race. . . .

All indications point to a bitter Congressional session, starting in January. (*Business Week,* 12 October 1957.[8])

■ SPUTNIK HARDENS KREMLIN'S LINE   The West has been reeling since early this month under the impact of Sputnik, with its revelation of the Soviet missile lead and the changed power balance in the world. Adding to the shock felt by every Western capital have been several Hitler-like blasts at the U.S. from Communist boss Nikita Khrushchev, threatening war in the Middle East. . . .

• Evil Omen—To the State Department, Sputnik immediately spelled real trouble ahead, the beginning of a period that might be as ticklish as the Korean War period, with danger possible in the Middle East and Berlin. Looking forward several years, State Department officials can see nothing but disaster for the U.S. unless we catch the Russians in the missile race.

. . . A top career diplomat, in an effort to put things in perspective, [said] "We still are ahead in nuclear weapons. Our deterrent power still is effective. But the balance of power is shifting against us fast. By 1960, if we don't make a total effort to catch up, we may be too weak either to negotiate a settlement or to prevent massive new Soviet expansion. Then the alternatives would be to capitulate or to fight a hydrogen war at a great disadvantage."

Such talk reflects a painful disillusionment in much of official Washington with the assumption of Soviet weakness that underlay our policy before Sputnik. . . .

There's no doubt that allied governments have been in a state of shock. Europeans in particular have been shaken by the immense power of blackmail that Sputnik has put into the hands of a ruthless fanatic like Khrushchev—and the impression among the underdeveloped countries that Communism can be efficient as well as powerful. (*Business Week,* 19 October 1957.[9])

■ SOVIETS PUT THEIR CHALLENGE INTO WORDS   For self exposure of the power-mad dictator, there has been nothing to match it (Khrushchev's interview by James Reston of *The New York Times*) since Hitler's *Mein Kampf.*

Almost everything is there, including the hysterical tone that the Fuehrer used when anybody stood in the way of an immediate goal. . . . Khrushchev has the same brazen way of turning the truth upside down, and of posing as a lover of peace. . . .

The Khrushchev interview isn't all bluster and bluff. The Soviet party boss put a lot of stress on his post-Sputnik terms for a deal with the U.S.

From the U.S., Khrushchev wants (1) full recognition of all existing Communist states; (2) acceptance of the U.S.S.R. as the protector of the Middle East; and (3) agreement to the disarmament and neutralization of West Germany. In return, he suggests that Moscow will consider an arms control deal and will generously recognize the right of the U.S., Britain, France, and a few other nations to maintain their capitalist systems. In short, this is a prescription for Soviet control of Europe and Asia, if not the entire world. . . .

What we face, quite clearly, is an even tougher struggle with Soviet Communism than we have known before. . . . (*Business Week,* 19 October 1957.[10])

■ INTERNATIONAL OUTLOOK   Syria's action (taking its dispute with Turkey to the U.N.) makes sense as a part of the war of nerves Khrushchev is waging. He's using the Soviet Union's lead in missiles as a starting point. Khrushchev's statements, couched in humiliating and provocative language, indicate that he believes he has already turned the tide of psychological warfare against the U.S. (*Business Week,* 19 October 1957.[11])

■ THE NATION WAITS FOR WASHINGTON   It is three weeks now since the Russians shot their artificial satellite into its pre-calculated orbit, thereby demonstrating that they had taken the lead in the race for new weapons. Three weeks should have been enough time for the U.S. to get over its initial shock and start facing up to the question of how it proposes to live in a new and unpleasant kind of world—a world in which it no longer has the protection of overwhelming superiority in technology.

So far, there is no indication that this imperative readjustment in the country's thinking is in progress. If anything, the public mind is more confused today than it was three weeks ago.

Much of this confusion in public thinking simply mirrors the confusion that is evident in the official statements that have been coming out of Washington. President Eisenhower, at his first press conference after the launching of Sputnik, declared that his concern about national defense had not been increased "one iota." White House Assistant Sherman Adams tried to dismiss it with a joke about basketballs. Various other figures in the Administration have argued that there never was a race with the Russians. . . .

Behind the scenes there is evidence of deep concern. The State Department is in a flap and will say so to anyone who asks how it feels about Sputnik and the Soviets' obvious intention of exploiting their advantage. . . . And from all over Washington, below the Cabinet level, there comes a flood of criticism and apprehensive prediction, obviously reflecting things that were said at some of the recent meetings of government officials and their scientific advisors so pointedly billed as "purely routine."

This is a bad situation. At best it gives the country an impression of uncertainty and vacillation in Washington. At worst, it looks like a head-in-the-sand refusal to admit that anything has happened. . . .

. . . U.S. defense policy, whether we have admitted it or not, has been based on the assumption that Russia was and always would be a second-rate industrial nation. The launching of Sputnik demonstrates with chilling finality that Russia not only has scientists equal to ours but that she has a highly developed and enormously capable industry to back them up.

There has been a severe shock to public confidence—as the violent reaction of the stock market testifies. . . .

Again and again throughout their history, the people of this country have shown a capacity for facing hard facts and accepting practical decisions. They will respond in the same way to the present emergency—if they are not encouraged to go back to sleep and forget the whole thing.

As we know now, it was a serious mistake to underrate the Russians. It would be an infinitely greater mistake at this point to underrate the people of the U.S. (*Business Week,* 26 October 1957.[12])

■ **WASHINGTON'S FIRST STEPS**   The first beginnings of a try by the United States and the Western Allies to regain parity with the Soviet Union in weapons are taking shape. . . . (*Business Week,* 26 October 1957.[13])

■ **INTERNATIONAL OUTLOOK**   President Eisenhower and British Prime Minister Macmillan are trying to reestablish something of the World War II alliance. This is their answer to (1) Sputnik and the rapid Soviet advance in military technology; and (2) the Kremlin's increasingly aggressive policy in the Middle East. . . . As U.S. and British officials see it, it is no longer just a case of Moscow fishing in troubled waters to see if its influence can be extended. Now it looks possible that Moscow may intend to blow the lid off in the Middle East. . . . (*Business Week,* 26 October 1957.[14])

■ **EDITORIAL**   At all costs we must now redress the military balance and avoid succumbing to the kind of blackmail that Hitler so successfully practiced on Europe in the Thirties.

. . . Russian theoretical science has proved itself superb. But with its very advance, Russian economics—the whole groaning apparatus of Marxism—is proving itself obsolete. (Editorial, *Fortune,* December, 1957, p. 113.)

■ **THE BATTLE OF DEFENSE BUILDS UP**   The second session of the 85th Congress opened this week on a note of crisis and urgency rarely felt in peacetime Washington. In the four months since Congress went home, the old international relationships have been shattered by a chain of events that are still shaking the foundations of U.S. military preparedness:

• Russia launched the first two earth satellites and forcibly demonstrated a technological lead over this country in ballistic missile development.

• The influential Gaither committee submitted a momentous report calling for a massive new arms buildup to counter Russia's growing military superiority.

• The Eisenhower Administration pulled a delayed but drastic policy switch, lifted its military budget ceilings, and set a new course for steep boosts in defense spending.

• The Senate preparedness subcommittee started a full-dress investigation of the missile program, generating a series of important proposals to overhaul the Pentagon.

. . . This week, there's no doubt that both Congress and the Administration are for a bigger and harder-driving defense buildup. . . . (*Business Week,* 11 January 1958.[15])

13
Why Do They Stay In This Business?

World Wars III and IV were lonely wars.

The two earlier ones involved total mobilization. Everyone knew there was a war going on. Information media were almost totally concerned about the war, and they gave strong support to America's defenders, including Rosie the Riveter. Practically everyone was involved, directly or indirectly.

World War III, by contrast, involved so few people that most of the others didn't realize it was going on. It lasted from 1954 to the mid-'60s, the period when ICBM's and other strategic offense and defense weapons were conceived, developed, produced, deployed and manned. It was lonely, manning a DEW-line outpost (distant early warning), standing a midnight watch, or sitting at a desk in a lab searching for answers to questions that had never been asked before.

Not many people understood what they were doing, because they were out of sight. This was a different kind of war.

Nevertheless it was exactly that. And for each side—

U.S. or U.S.S.R.—that developed a strategic system or introduced changes, the other side calculated the effect and developed a means to offset the advantage. Computers were called on to evaluate the weight that should be given to each change and to keep score on each side's position. It cost a lot of sweat and money; but it was sweat and money, rather than blood, sweat, tears and money.

World War IV began in the mid-'60s, with more sophisticated electronic and space systems, and more advanced means of deployment and logistic support. Technology became an increasingly important source of national power.

Defense for these two wars was tremendously expensive; but the weapons and support systems developed for them succeeded, by the very fact that they did not have to be used. In a sense, because they weren't used up, they were wasted; but they served their purpose in deterring a global conflict. As technology progressed, they became obsolete and had to be replaced by newer weapons, a characteristic of today's technology in general.

At the same time it was necessary for the military and industry to support a major effort in Vietnam, to provide backing for an individual described in this way by a senior commander there:

> Today's young soldier is a splendid soldier. Independent, imaginative, critical, inquisitive, self-sacrificing, mature and brave—that's him.
>
> But when one considers him in the context of our times, he is even more marvelous! He is fighting a tough and cunning enemy whom he must come to appreciate and master, almost at arm's length. He is fighting in a quite unpleasant environment, foreign to his experience of relative comfort and sophistication. He is placing his life in the hands of junior

combat leaders not much more experienced and certainly little older than he. He is participating in a war that is probably neither supported nor understood by his loved ones. He is willing to lay his life on the line for an eventual outcome that is quite unclear to him and, apparently, to many of his political leaders.

But this quick-grown teen-age *man* is a professional in every respect. He "humps it" in the jungle for months on end without anything more serious than a soldierly gripe. He defends "his wire" under intensive human wave attacks made by little people he neither understands nor hates. He calmly drinks his warm coke, flips his cigarette butt, and hops on the floor of a chopper to fly off to some stinking hole in a jungle called an LZ (Landing Zone) to face whatever challenge awaits him there.

He is a professional soldier, and he is a strong American citizen. Somehow he senses that what he is doing is right and worthwhile. No matter what the outcome of this war for us, we all can be proud of him and thankful for his strength and faith in our future.

The job of providing the equipment and supplies for both the war that warmed up, and for The Loneliest War fell to the military-industrial complex. MIC alone fought the lonely one. Most of the rest of us didn't even know it was going on. We would have found out with a bang if it had been less successful.

THE REASONS FOR MIC

The U.S. and the rest of the Western World have consistently underrated the Russians and the Chinese, in both their intent and their capabilities. Sputnik is only one example of the reasons for MIC. From a standing start, the U.S.S.R. developed nuclear weapons far sooner than anyone had expected, even with the help of subversives. Then they demonstrated a bomber force capable of delivering them.

At a time when some in this country were crowing about how far ahead U.S. technology was vis-à-vis the Russians', they caught us flat-footed with Sputnik. They showed, without a doubt, that they had not only a much further-advanced rocket propulsion capability, but also the guidance and control system for a sophisticated intercontinental ballistic missile system. The U.S., with a crash program and sudden reversal of defense cutbacks, produced an ICBM with limited operational capability two years later. But we couldn't know whether these soft, exposed missiles were under attack until there *was* an attack, when it would be too late to use them. So we built ballistic missile early-warning stations at Clear, Alaska and Thule, Greenland to detect, shortly after launching, missiles that might be launched from Asia.

This raised the question of what happens if, instead of launching a salvo over the polar regions, the U.S.S.R. lobs one that takes the long way home—around the *South* polar region, for instance? Fortunately this didn't require much serious attention, because the capability to do this didn't exist.

But then along came FOBS, the fractional orbit bombardment system, designed to do just that—to travel a fraction of an earth's orbit from launch to a pre-designated impact point, without ever being detected. And meanwhile the U.S.S.R. developed *and tested* a far larger nuclear weapon (a sixty-megaton bomb) than the U.S. has ever produced, tested an anti-ballistic missile system *eight years ago,* and brought out highly advanced fighter aircraft about every two years. (The basic design of the U.S.' last operational fighter, the F-4 Phantom, was "frozen" in 1955.)

Red China, too, developed a nuclear capability much sooner than either the U.S. or U.S.S.R. believed possible. But it still didn't have the means of delivering it, and former Defense Secretary McNamara believed they wouldn't have the means for a long time. Then the Chinese began developing missiles, and now they are many years closer to having a nuclear missile capability than anyone believed possible two years ago.

These are indications of the capabilities.

As to intent, our foresight isn't nearly so clear as hindsight. But former Secretary of State Dean Acheson, speaking before a subcommittee of the Joint Economic Committee of Congress, said:

> I see no basis for the notion that we tend to overdo the military aspects. To the contrary, the nation has repeatedly neglected to provide a military basis to match its policy or to cope with aggressive forces. We tried unilateral arms reduction in the interwar period. We got Pearl Harbor. We reverted to habit after World War II. We got the Korean War. With respect to military power, I do not share the worries of those who discern and deplore dangers of too much. . . .
>
> In former times we could count on time and distance as safety factors. That situation has vanished, probably forever. The development has not been due to some correctible error of judgment and practice on our part. The determining factors are the disintegration of the Europe-centered world, the establishment of a great power base for revolutionary purposes with universal ambitions, and the dynamism of technology.
>
> From here on, as far ahead as one can imagine, the nation will continuously be in the front line, and coping with adversary forces will be an unrelenting requirement.

For some among us, it is hard to get accustomed to the new circumstances. The temptation is
to take the old situation as normal, to regard the huge
expense and unremitting danger as aberrant, and to
blame or malign . . . forces within our own establishment.[1]

Mr. Acheson has also commented on the Communist
use of negotiations as a means of gaining their ends, of using
time to best advantage. On the other hand, W. Averell Harri-
man, former chief negotiator at the Paris peace talks says, "Our
security will not come from the number of our weapons. It will
come from the strength of our moral force at home and abroad,
from our economic and social strength, and from the unity of
our people."[2]

But *when*?

When Mark Twain was seventeen, he thought his dad
was a real square. When he was twenty-one, he was amazed
how much the old man had picked up in four years.

When the U.S.S.R. was younger, it probably had similar
feelings; as that country matures, maybe it is finding out that
living in the same world with the U.S. isn't so bad after all. But
China, for all its ancient history, is a long way from becoming
a teen-ager. When it hits twenty-one, then may be the time for
moral force and economic and social strength to hold sway.
No one would be more pleased than our military. But until we
arrive one day at that point, World War IV seems the best way
to ensure that we *do* arrive at that point, and arrive there without detouring through an intervening general war.

Meanwhile, the cost will continue to be great, corresponding to our global responsibilities. Eight percent or more
of our total production of goods and services will go into defense. But the U.S.S.R. devotes about 20 percent of its gross

national product to defense, even without direct involvement in a hassle like Vietnam. The U.S.S.R. is not so much a military-industrial complex as it is a military-industrial state.

The best defense of MIC, if it needs one, is its record: it performs. It has never failed to produce the equipment and weaponry required, however advanced technologically and in whatever quantities required. But in the past it has had time to get reoriented; the premium now, like never before, is on time. For this reason, an industrial capacity *in being* and producing is mandatory. This in itself is a large deterrent, as General Douglas MacArthur recognized in his address to the National Association of Manufacturers in December, 1954:

> The successful conduct of a military campaign now depends upon industrial supremacy. As a consequence, the Armed Forces of a nation and its industrial power have become one and inseparable. The integration of the leadership of one into the leadership of the other is not only logical but inescapable. It has become indisputably clear that it is no longer the standing Armies now in being, nor the Naval and Air Forces which range freedom's vast frontiers, which stay the bloody specter of willful aggression, but rather a realistic appreciation of our massive potential of industrial power which is so capable of rapidly mounting the means to retaliate and to destroy. Industry has thus become the leavening influence in a world where war and the threat and fear of war would otherwise distort the minds of men and violently react upon the peaceful progress of the human race.

But as one writer points out, "The Russians doubt not our capacity; they doubt our will." And a Radio Hanoi broadcast on October 13 and 14, 1969 exults, "The present autumn struggle wave of the American people is putting the Nixon Administration into a very difficult and confused situation. . . . The Vietnamese people heartily welcome and entirely support the October wave of struggle. The whole world is standing on your side and acting in coordination with you."

THE MILITARY-INDUSTRIAL RELATIONSHIP

Here's how the military-industrial relationship, in its LEEPSMIC configuration, looks to an outsider. J.-J. Servan-Schreiber, editor of Paris' *L'Express,* and the American economist he quotes, with rare discernment, praise the effectiveness of the Government-business-engineer/scientist-educator complex, the "technostructure" that presents both an industrial challenge to Western Europe and a defense challenge to would-be aggressors:

> During the *past ten years,* from the end of the cold war and the launching of the first Sputnik, American power has made an unprecedented leap forward. . . . In America today, the government official, the industrial manager, the economics professor, the engineer and the scientist have joined forces to develop coordinated techniques for integrating factors of production.[3]

Servan-Schreiber notes that these techniques amount to an industrial revolution whose originality lies in this fusion of talents. John K. Galbraith calls this remarkably effective combination of forces a "technostructure."

Servan-Schreiber also comments on the compression of time from invention to manufacture of new products:[4]

Photography	112 years (1727-1839)
Telephone	56 years (1820-1876)
Radio	35 years (1867-1902)
Radar	15 years (1925-1940)
Television	12 years (1922-1934)
Atomic bomb	6 years (1939-1945)
Transistor	5 years (1948-1953)
Integrated circuits	3 years (1958-1961)

"The development of new products," he says, "has reached a momentum undreamed of before the war, or even ten years ago."

In a reference to the advanced technological environment of the military-industrial complex, the author's fellow countryman, Pierre Cognard, said after a visit to the United States, "Accustomed to work in technical fields which pose far broader problems than those of the commercial market, and aided by the government contracts, American firms are now developing industrial and technological methods far more advanced than anything in Europe."

American industry's capability of accepting and mastering change, and its virtuosity in management, are well recognized by those in an objective position to judge its effectiveness. Given clear goals, a challenge, and adequate backing, LEEPS-MIC could even put a man on the moon.

The triumph of high achievement in the latter half of the twentieth century generally results from a fusion of talents. The fundamental nature of the relationship between contractors and the Government is a fiduciary one: the industrial tiger fighter is a trustee for managing a program toward its technical, cost, and schedule objectives. During the competition phase and negotiations, of course, the relationship is one of tough,

tooth-and-nail bargaining on each side. But after the contract
terms are hammered out, the relationship must be one of working together to solve a difficult problem; closeness is absolutely
necessary between technical and management people in defining the problem in precise terms, and in developing solutions.
This requires the best possible skills and experience; and it is
for this reason that retired and former Government defense
people are employed in industry.

LAST OF THE GREAT CONTRACTORS

"What business should we be in?" This is a fundamental question raised in well-managed companies, in whatever
industry. It's a question that doesn't come up just one time and
is answered only once; it recurs periodically, and the answer
changes, just as technology changes.

The danger in the military-industrial complex is that the
reasons for going into other lines of business may outweigh the
reasons for staying in the defense business. No one recognizes
this better than America's competition.

Armed Services Procurement Regulation 3-808.1 says:

> ... Effective national defense in a free enterprise
> economy requires that the best industrial capabilities
> be attracted to defense contracts. These capabilities
> will be driven away from the defense market if de-
> fense contracts are characterized by low profit oppor-
> tunities. Consequently, negotiations aimed merely at
> reducing prices by reducing profits, with no realiza-
> tion of the function of profit, cannot be condoned....

Even the Comptroller General of the United States says,
"However, we believe it is important that profits be sufficient to

maintain a healthy defense industry and encourage contractors to undertake Government work and provide them with financial incentives to perform in an efficient and economical manner."[5]

But profit has declined. Regulations and paper work have become more burdensome. Risks have grown much greater. Unjustified criticism, along with some that is justified, runs rampant.

Companies, like individuals, like to be appreciated and to go where they're appreciated.

The question recurs again and again: why do they stay in this business? Some of the answers are these: there's the challenge in meeting tough requirements, the excitement in new fields of tiger fighting, the tradition of achievement; it's the kind of business they do best. And at a time when patriotism is a word mocked and ridiculed by many who enjoy the fruits, without the effort, of others' beliefs, patriotism is a reason.

But these reasons may not be good enough in the future to "attract the best industrial capabilities" to defense work. Even now the trend among many defense contractors is away from defense business: greater diversification into commercial business, for instance, and mergers with commercial/industrial firms to reduce the risks and accordion-effect of Government business while passing on their technological expertise to merger partners. Ten years ago the aerospace industry was 90 percent military and 10 percent commercial. Now the commercial market is about 40 percent of the total. The danger in shaking capable firms out of producing for defense is that it's so permanent. Its effect would require years to reverse—in a period when the value of time is immense, and increasing. Dr. John S. Foster, Jr., Director of Defense Research and Engineering, warns that "the U.S. in the future may well see superiority in defense technology pass to the Soviet Union." The decline of our industrial capability would be a huge gash in the country's protective umbrella.

Companies who have been in the defense business for a long time, a dozen years or more, are real pro's in their field. And this is the problem. Bill Russell of Boston's peerless Celtics expressed it well:

> If you're really looking for a reason why I feel I've played enough, I'll tell you this. There are professionals and there are mercenaries in sports. The difference between them is that the professional is involved. I was never a mercenary. If I continued to play, I'd become a mercenary because I'm not involved anymore. . . . But I'm not going to play basketball for money. I've been paid to play, of course, but I played for a lot of other reasons, too.
>
> I played because I enjoyed it—but there's more to it than that. I played because I was dedicated to being the best. I was part of a team and I dedicated myself to making that team the best. To me, one of the most beautiful things to see is a group of men coordinating their efforts toward a common goal—alternately subordinating and asserting themselves to achieve real teamwork in action. I tried to do that —we all tried to do that—on the Celtics. I think we succeeded. Often, in my mind's eye, I stood off and watched that effort. I found it beautiful to watch. It's just as beautiful to watch in things other than sports.[6]

In defense contracting, a company *has* to be "involved"; otherwise its objective is effort, rather than accomplishment. It becomes a drone, motivated not to being the best and accomplishing the most, but to being paid for effort, whether the effort produces results or not.

In spite of the need for attracting the best firms to defense production, one Senator says: "The wise industrialists now, therefore, are not those who focus their long-range planning on the military money tree. On the contrary, they are concerned with the ability of their enterprise to convert to other pursuits: to operate in a civilian economy. Unfortunately, those who are planning along these lines are few and far between."[7] Even more unfortunately, an increasing number *are* planning along these lines. And when only one-sixth of the total business of the twenty-five largest contractors is in defense, it is clear that they can do without defense business a lot easier than Defense can do without them as contractors.

So soon do many supporters of the late President Kennedy, now among MIC's bitterest critics, forget the words of his Inaugural Address:

> We dare not tempt them with weakness. For only when our arms are sufficient beyond doubt can we be certain beyond doubt that they will never be employed.

And his statement:

> I believe that there can only be one possible defense policy for the United States. It can be expressed in one word. That word is *first*. I do not mean first, but. I do not mean first, when. I do not mean first, if. I mean first—period.

CONCLUSION

Maybe the wise ones will depart the arena of tigers and tiger fighters, as Senator McGovern suggests, and find greener fields. Maybe it's time for a moral force to go into the game instead of a military force; maybe it's time for Broadway Joe, Cassius Clay, SDSers and other outstanding believers in the individual's rights to take over. It would be a lot cheaper than the cost of defense, which is almost twice what the U.S. will spend this year on new cars. And it would still be a while before the award is made for winning second place in a military contest.

As the line-up changes, a PA system blares, "The Jefferson Airplane is now batting for Lockheed. They'll be followed in the clean-up spot by the McGuire Sisters singing 'Sugartime.'"

Appendix

I

THE PROPOSAL
EVALUATION PROCESS

With the increasing complexity of systems development, the process for evaluating contractors' proposals and for source selection has been steadily refined and systematized. The technique used by the Army Material Command (AMC), described here, is generally similar to techniques used in other procurement organizations in the Department of Defense. The purpose of these techniques is to assure both the Service and industry that proposals are judged with objectivity, competence, and integrity.

The basic components of a source selection system are

Organizing for the evaluation
Determining the evaluation criteria
Scoring each part of each proposal
Assigning weight factors to elements of the proposal.

Source: Victor Garvis, "Contractor Proposal Evaluation Process Defined by AMC," *Defense Industry Bulletin*, August 1969, pp. 15-18.

ORGANIZING THE EVALUATION TEAM

The request for proposal (RFP) issued to competing bidders establishes the format for the contractor's proposal, and consequently establishes the structure of the evaluation team. A chairman and his staff direct the efforts of the organization in carrying out the evaluation tasks. The second level of the organization is composed of groups who correspond to the major sections of the RFP; for instance, groups are established to evaluate the technical management and cost areas. These groups in turn are composed of committees who are identified with smaller segments of the RFP. The technical group, for example, may be segmented into a vehicle committee, a propulsion committee, an armament committee, and other committees. Depending on the complexity of the system, subcommittees or sub-subcommittees may be established.

Individuals selected for evaluating proposals are chosen with extreme care, based on their talent, professional accomplishments, experience, personal integrity and reputation, and ability to exercise good judgment. Members generally are relieved of all other duties in order that they will be able to devote their full attention to completing the task within a tight time frame. There is no room for error in any part of the evaluation.

EVALUATION CRITERIA

The evaluation criteria are developed before receiving the proposals from contractors. Often, in fact, they are developed prior to *issuing* the RFP, in order to test the logic and completeness of responses required of the contractors.

Figure 1 shows one basis for scoring and evaluation. This criteria channels the proposal review directly to specific items or areas. As shown in Figure 1, a typical evaluation statement is "sequential logic of network events" (referring to the logic of the PERT or CPM network), or "special test equipment cost for high risk areas."

Upon receipt of proposals from competing bidders, the criteria are "locked in" and changes are not allowed.

SCORING

The evaluation method includes a scoring system for rating the merit of each proposal. Contractors' responses are scored for the degree of excellence related to each item of the evaluation criteria.

Individual ratings by the evaluator are "raw" or unweighted scores, and typically are based on a range from 10 to 0 as follows:

10   *Outstanding:* A comprehensive and extensive response in depth, displaying a very high degree of capability in a respective area.

9   *Superior:* An extensive and detailed response to all requirements, displaying high-level capability in a respective area.

8   *Excellent:* A response with clearly definable detailed information for all major positions of requirement, with a strong capability in excess of the basic requirement.

EVALUATION PYRAMID

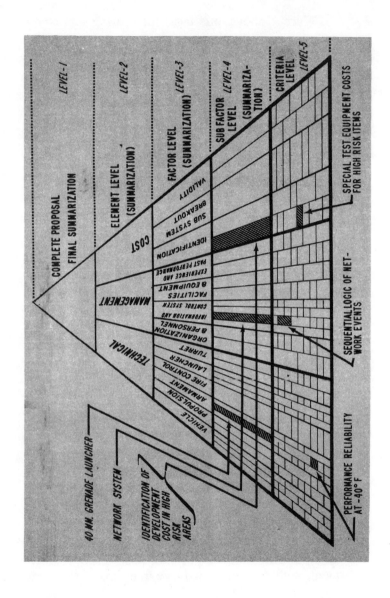

Figure 1.

7   *Very Good:* A response with detailed information and recognized capability in excess of minimum requirements in a respective area.

6   *Good:* A response with limited detail and capability in excess of the minimum requirement in a respective area.

5   *Adequate:* A response complying with the established requirements, with acceptable capability in a respective area.

4   *Weak:* Lack of clarity in a response or vague indications that a capability exists.

3   *Poor:* Omission of minor details—omissions or misunderstandings of requirements in a minor area of capability not defined.

2   *Very Poor:* Omission of major details and facts—omission of major requirements or misunderstandings of major requirements in a respective area.

1   *Inadequate:* Gross omissions or failure to respond to a major requirement.

0   *Nonresponsive:* Failure to submit data in a given area.

Scoring is accomplished by evaluators on an individual basis, independent of other evaluators. Original basic scores assigned by an evaluator are not modified by any other individual; questions concerning an original basic score may be brought to the evaluator's attention, but he alone can make a change or correction.

Each individual score is supported by a narrative justification outlining the strong and weak points. These narratives may vary from two or three sentences to several pages in length.

WEIGHTING

Some areas of a proposal for complex weapon systems warrant greater emphasis than do other parts. The Vasa incident, in Chapter 11, illustrates the reasons for this. Normally, as shown in Figure 2, the technical proposal bears greater weight than the management and cost proposals, for the reason that it doesn't make any difference how well managed and how under-cost the project is if the hardware fails to perform.

Figure 2 illustrates how weights might be assigned to each level of the evaluation pyramid.

Weight information is not disclosed to evaluation groups until all scores have been assigned and narrative justifications have been completed.

WEIGHT ASSIGNMENTS

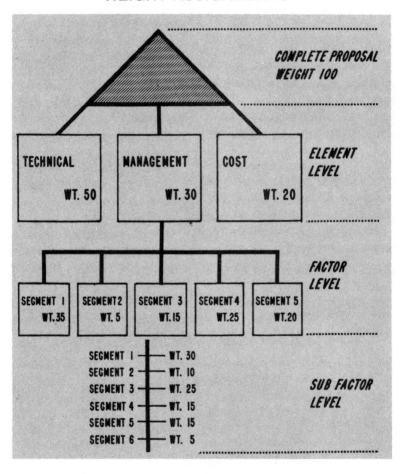

Figure 2.

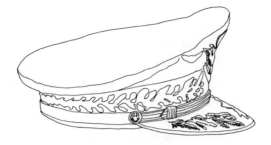

II

DUTY, HONOR, COUNTRY

As I was leaving the hotel this morning, a doorman asked me, "Where are you bound for, General?" and when I replied, "West Point," he remarked, "Beautiful place, have you ever been there before?"

No human being could fail to be deeply moved by such a tribute as this. (Thayer Award). Coming from a profession I have served so long and a people I have loved so well, it fills me with an emotion I cannot express. But this award is not intended primarily for a personality, but to symbolize a great moral code —the code of conduct and chivalry of those who guard this beloved land of culture and ancient descent.

Source: General of the Army Douglas MacArthur's address to the Corps of Cadets at West Point on May 12, 1962, on his receiving the Sylvanus Thayer Medal for service to his country, the highest honor of the United States Military Academy. General MacArthur literally spoke "from the heart"; he had no prepared text or even notes. From a tape recording, however, *The National Observer* was able to present his farewell address to the Corps in its issue of May 20, 1962. The address is reproduced here by permission of *The National Observer*.

Duty, honor, country: Those three hallowed words reverently dictate what you ought to be, what you can be, what you will be. They are your rallying point to build courage when courage seems to fail, to regain faith when there seems to be little cause for faith, to create hope when hope becomes forlorn.

Unhappily, I possess neither that eloquence of diction, that poetry of imagination, nor that brilliance of metaphor to tell you all that they mean.

The unbelievers will say they are but words, but a slogan, but a flamboyant phrase. Every pedant, every demagogue, every cynic, every hypocrite, every troublemaker, and, I am sorry to say, some others of an entirely different character, will try to downgrade them even to the extent of mockery and ridicule.

But these are some of the things they build. They build your basic character. They mold you for your future roles as the custodians of the nation's defense. They make you strong enough to know when you are weak, and brave enough to face yourself when you are afraid.

What the Words Teach

They teach you to be proud and unbending in honest failure, but humble and gentle in success; not to substitute words for actions, nor to seek the path of comfort, but to face the stress and spur of difficulty and challenge; to learn to stand up in the storm, but to have compassion on those who fall; to master yourself before you seek to master others; to have a heart that is clean, a goal that is high; to learn to laugh, yet never forget how to weep; to reach into the future, yet never neglect the past; to be serious, yet never to take yourself too seriously; to be modest so that you will remember the simplicity of true greatness; the open mind of true wisdom, the meekness of true strength.

They give you a temperate will, a quality of imagination, a vigor of the emotions, a freshness of the deep springs of life, a temperamental predominance of courage over timidity, an appetite for adventure over love of ease.

They create in your heart the sense of wonder, the unfailing hope of what next, and the joy and inspiration of life. They teach you in this way to be an officer and a gentleman.

And what sort of soldiers are those you are to lead? Are they reliable? Are they brave? Are they capable of victory?

Their story is known to all of you. It is the story of the American man at arms. My estimate of him was formed on the battlefield many, many years ago, and has never changed. I regarded him then, as I regard him now, as one of the world's noblest figures; not only as one of the finest military characters, but also as one of the most stainless.

His name and fame are the birthright of every American citizen. In his youth and strength, his love and loyalty, he gave all that mortality can give. He needs no eulogy from me, or from any other man. He has written his own history and written it in red on his enemy's breast. . . .

Witness to the Fortitude

In twenty campaigns, on a hundred battlefields, around a thousand camp fires, I have witnessed that enduring fortitude, that patriotic self-abnegation, and that invincible determination which have carved his stature in the hearts of his people.

From one end of the world to the other, he has drained deep the chalice of courage. As I listened to those songs of the glee club, in memory's eyes I could see those staggering columns of the first World War, bending under soggy packs on many a weary march, from dripping dusk to drizzling dawn, slogging ankle deep through mire of shell-pocked roads; to form grimly for the attack, blue-lipped, covered with sludge and mud, chilled by the wind and rain, driving home to their objective, and for many, to the judgment seat of God. . . .

I do not know the dignity of their birth, but I do know the glory of their death. They died unquestioning, uncomplaining, with faith in their hearts, and on their lips the hope that we would go on to victory.

Always for them: Duty, honor, country. Always their blood, sweat, and tears, as we sought the way and the light. And twenty years after, on the other side of the globe, again the filth of murky foxholes, the stench of ghostly trenches, the slime of dripping dugouts, those boiling suns of the relentless heat, those torrential rains of devastating storms, the loneliness and utter desolation of jungle trails, the bitterness of long separation from those they loved and cherished, the deadly pestilence of tropical disease, the horror of stricken areas of war.

Swift and Sure Attack

Their resolute and determined defense, their swift and sure attack, their indomitable purpose, their complete and decisive victory—always victory, always through the bloody haze of their last reverberating shot, the vision of gaunt, ghastly men, reverently following your password of Duty, honor, country. . . .

You now face a new world, a world of change. The thrust into outer space of the satellite, spheres, and missiles marks a beginning of another epoch in the long story of mankind. In the five or more billions of years the scientist tell us it has taken to form the earth, in the three or more billion years of development of the human race, there has never been a greater, a more abrupt or staggering evolution.

We deal now, not with things of this world alone, but with the illimitable distances and as yet unfathomed mysteries of the universe. We are reaching out for a new and boundless frontier. We speak in strange terms of harnessing the cosmic energy, of making winds and tides work for us . . . of the primary target in war, no longer limited to the armed forces of an enemy, but instead to include his civil populations; of ultimate conflict between a united human race and the sinister forces of some other planetary galaxy; of such dreams and fantasies as to make life the most exciting of all times.

And through all this welter of change and development your mission remains fixed, determined, inviolable. It is to win our wars. Everything else in your professional career is but corollary to this vital dedication. All other public purposes, all other public projects, all other public needs, great or small, will find others for their accomplishment; but you are the ones who are trained to fight.

The Profession of Arms

Yours is the profession of arms, the will to win, the sure knowledge that in war there is no substitute for victory, that if you lose, the nation will be destroyed, that the very obsession of your public service must be Duty, honor, country.

Others will debate the controversial issues, national and international, which divide men's minds. But serene, calm, aloof, you stand as the nation's war guardians, as its lifeguards from the raging tides of international conflict, as its gladiators in the arena of battle. For a century and a half you have defended, guarded, and protected its hallowed traditions of liberty and freedom, of right and justice.

Let civilian voices argue the merits or demerits of our processes of government: whether our strength is being sapped by deficit financing indulged in too long, by Federal paternalism grown too mighty, by power groups grown too arrogant, by politics grown too corrupt, by crime grown too rampant, by morals grown too low, by taxes grown too high, by extremists grown too violent; whether our personal liberties are as thorough and complete as they should be.

These great national problems are not for your professional participation or military solution. Your guidepost stands out like a tenfold beacon in the night: Duty, honor, country.

You are the leaven which binds together the entire fabric of our national system of defense. From your ranks come the great captains who hold the nation's destiny in their hands the moment the war tocsin sounds. . . .

The long gray line has never failed us. Were you to do so, a million ghosts in olive drab, in brown khaki, in blue and gray, would rise from their white crosses, thundering those magic words: Duty, honor, country.

Prays for Peace

This does not mean that you are warmongers. On the contrary, the soldier above all other people prays for peace, for he must suffer and bear the deepest wounds and scars of war. But always in our ears ring the ominous words of Plato, that wisest of all philosophers: "Only the dead have seen the end of war."

The shadows are lengthening for me. The twilight is here. My days of old have vanished—tone and tint. They have gone glimmering through the dreams of things that were. Their memory is one of wondrous beauty, watered by tears and coaxed and caressed by the smiles of yesterday. I listen vainly, but with thirsty ear, for the witching melody of faint bugles blowing reveille, of far drums beating the long roll.

In my dreams I hear again the crash of guns, the rattle of musketry, the strange, mournful mutter of the battlefield. But in the evening of my memory always I come back to West Point. Always there echoes and re-echoes: Duty, honor, country.

Today marks my final roll call with you. But I want you to know that when I cross the river, my last conscious thoughts will be of the corps, and the corps, and the corps.

I bid you farewell.

THE ENTERPRISE
OF THE INDIES

In 1491, their Royal Majesties Ferdinand and Isabella, by the Grace of God King and Queen of Castile, Leon, Aragon, Sicily, etc., etc., were up to their royal ears in strife. The King had assembled the flower of Spanish knighthood in his efforts to supplant the Moorish crescent with the cross in Granada, and was directing the siege from a fortified camp erected outside the city. Preoccupied though he was, Ferdinand nevertheless took time to receive one Cristobal Colon, again. He knew why Colon had come to his headquarters.

Six years earlier the King and Queen had received this same Colon and listened to his request for royal patronage for an Enterprise of the Indies. They referred his ideas and propositions to a special commission of "learned men and mariners." After four years of deliberation and efforts to learn more specifically what Colon had in mind, the commission returned

Source: A case prepared by James H. Carbone and Daniel J. Strauss.

its findings. As might have been predicted, Columbus' request was denied on the grounds that (1) a voyage to Asia would require three years; (2) the Western Ocean is infinite and perhaps unnavigable; (3) if he reached the Antipodes (the land on the other side of the globe from Europe), he could not get back; (4) there are no Antipodes because the greater part of the globe is covered with water and because Saint Augustine said so; (5) of the five zones, only three are habitable; (6) so many centuries after the Creation, it was unlikely that anyone could find hitherto unknown lands of any value.

Ferdinand nevertheless had meanwhile ordered municipal and local officials to furnish free board and lodging to "Cristobal Colon who has come to our court." With this support, and being lodged and fed at public expense, Columbus persisted in his enterprise, in spite of the learned commission's findings. Now he was at Santa Fe, the camp where the king was directing the siege, to press for royal backing.

Early in 1492 the siege of Granada was won "by the cross," and with the collapse of the Moorish kingdom, Ferdinand had an opportunity to weigh Columbus' request. The result: request denied again.

Columbus resolved to go to France for the support he needed and "to bestow the glory and riches of his expedition upon a receptive monarch." But enroute to France he was intercepted by a royal messenger. Queen Isabella had been persuaded by supporters of Columbus to back his enterprise—at least in part by the rationale that a small investment could bring great returns. After three additional months of discussions and administrative delay, Columbus obtained the necessary royal support.

On Wednesday, 23 May 1492, "in the church of St. George of this town of Palos, in the presence of Fr. Juan Perez and of the mayor and councilors, Cristobal Colon gave and presented to the aforesaid the following letter of their Highnesses, the which is read by me, Francisco Fernandes, notary public of said Town:

> "Ferdinand and Isabella, by the Grace of God King and Queen of Castile, Leon, Aragon, Sicily, Etc., to you Diego Rodriguez Prieto and all the other inhabitants of the town of Palos, greeting and grace.
>
> "Know ye that whereas for certain things done and committed by you to our disservice you were condemned and obligated by our Council to provide for us a twelvemonth with two equipped caravels at your own proper charge and expense. . . . And whereas we have now commanded Cristobal Colon to go with three *carabelas de armada* as our Captain of same, toward certain regions of the Ocean Sea, to perform certain things for our service, and we desire that he take with him the said two caravels with which you are thus required to serve us; therefore we command that within six weeks of receiving this our letter . . . you have all ready and prepared two equipped caravels, as you are required by virtue of the said sentence, to depart with the said Cristobal Colon whither we have commanded him to go . . . and we have commanded him to give you advance pay for four months for the people who are to sail aboard the said caravels at the rate to be paid to the other people who are to be in the said three [sic] caravels, and in the other caravel that we have commanded him to take, whatever is commonly and customarily paid on this coast to the people who go to sea in a fleet. . . ."
>
> "Given in our City of Granada on the 30th day of April, year of our Lord Jesus Christ 1492."

The town fathers, who were held responsible for complying with the sentence served upon Palos promptly resolved any ambiguity in the royal letter by establishing the following statement of work:

> Supply two caravel ships (not three).
> Supply reconditioning services and provisions for a voyage to "certain regions of the Ocean Sea," i.e., the Orient.
> Provide crews for the two caravel ships.
> Complete such preparations *in forty-two days.*

The mayor of Palos, who would be personally guilty of compounded "disservices" if the caravel project went awry, petitioned their Majesties for an extension of the preparation period to allow an additional thirty days. Over the objections of Admiral Columbus, who wanted to avoid any royal change of mind that might terminate his adventure before it started, the petition was granted, subject to presenting to their Majesties' representative an acceptable rationale (master milestone chart) clearly identifying the work to be performed, scheduling of the work, and an explanation of why the additional time would be required.

Due to delays in coordination, delays in sending messages back and forth, and delays in preliminary planning, actual work on the project did not start until June 24. By then, only forty days remained in which to complete the work before the scheduled sailing.

Meanwhile, in order to meet the difficult schedule, chandlers, shipwrights, sailmakers, timber merchants, cartographers, bakers, physicians, metalsmiths, chronologers, caulkers, coopers, compass makers and others were designated to contribute their special skills in the preparations. Each realized that his support was required as penalty for Palos' "disservice" to Ferdinand and Isabella.

PROJECT TASKS

Preparation for The Enterprise of the Indies involved three major tasks.

CARAVEL TASK

Each caravel was to have a crew of twenty-five seamen and officers. Each had a carrying capacity of fifty-one tons. By direction of Admiral Columbus, the equipage was not to include armament, since the voyage was for exploration rather than conquest. All available space was to be used for provisions and marine equipment. Specifications were:

> Dimensions: twenty-three feet beam, fifty feet keel length, seventy feet overall length.
>
> Draft: six feet.
>
> Structure: one deck; raised quarterdeck containing masters cabin; small, low forecastle for storage of cables, sail locker, bread room, firebox, etc.
>
> Rigging: Genoa model; three-masted lateener; mainmast having the longest yard, almost amidships; two other masts aft.
>
> Speed: Although maximum speed could rise to eight knots under the most favorable conditions, average speed for familiar waters was closer to two knots.

CREW TASK

Notwithstanding the perils of the voyage on the uncharted Ocean Sea, a capable crew had to be recruited and signed on. All civil and criminal prosecutions were to be suspended against anyone who agreed to ship with Admiral Columbus. The fleet required a total of thirty officers and sixty seamen.

PROVISIONING TASK

Provisioning posed a problem. Provisions were available from the citizens of Palos by royal command, but how much provisioning would be needed? How long would the voyage to the Indies require? Since the carrying capacity of the caravel was limited, the right mix of provisions, materials, equipment and supplies would have to be selected to sustain twenty-five crewmen and officers for an indeterminate period, under unknown sailing conditions, for each of the two caravels.

WORK BREAKDOWN STRUCTURE

As a first step in organizing the myriad activities involved, a work breakdown structure was prepared, as shown in Figure 1.

NETWORK SCHEDULING

The Mayor of Palos sought a means to assure himself that his tenure as Mayor and his liberty would not be terminated. He resolved that he could control the caravel project only by using the latest technique in overseeing complex enterprises: "La Evaluacion de Programa Y Technica de Revista" (PERT). He recognized that he could perform the tasks for the two ships simultaneously, so that the master milestone schedule and PERT network for one ship would serve the other also.

A network of activities, like that in Figure 2, was prepared to show the various activities and to determine interdependencies and the critical path.

The critical path showed that fifty-three days would be required, unless changes were made to reduce the time required for preparation. It was clear that risks in recruiting officers and seamen were necessary, even though the quality of the crew

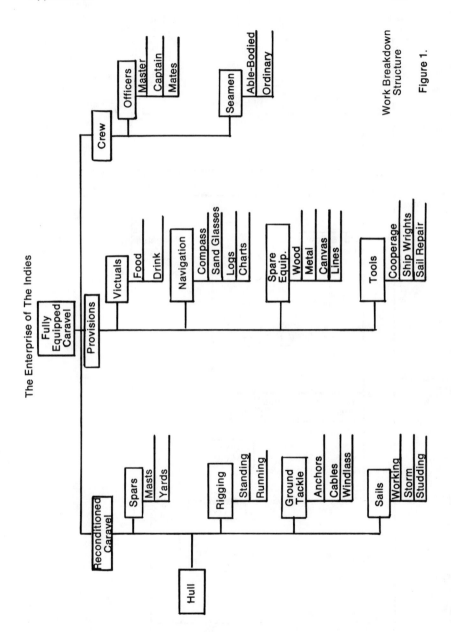

The Enterprise of The Indies

Work Breakdown Structure

Figure 1.

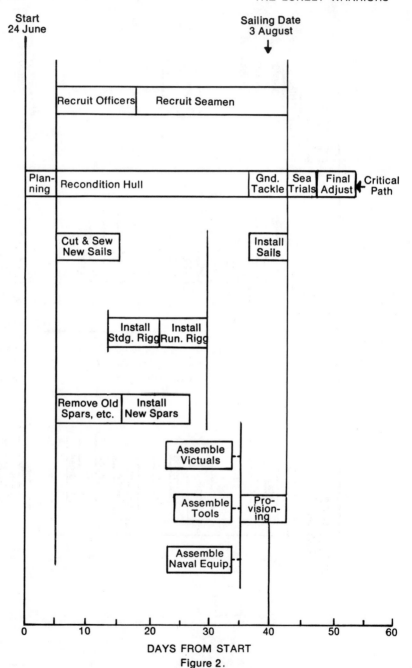

Figure 2.

would suffer. Reconditioning the hull would also have to be done in less time; it was decided that working at night as well as daytime would be necessary to shorten the reconditioning period. And Admiral Columbus agreed, reluctantly, to shorten the time for sea trials from seven days to three days.

Finally, a revised network was developed that looked like the one in Figure 3.

If all went as planned, the caravels would be ready for the voyage within forty days. Based on this, the sailing was set for early on the morning of August 3.

It was expected that additional provisioning could be obtained at San Sebastian in the Canary Islands. Thereafter there was only the unknown, and the dread of falling off the edge of the world.

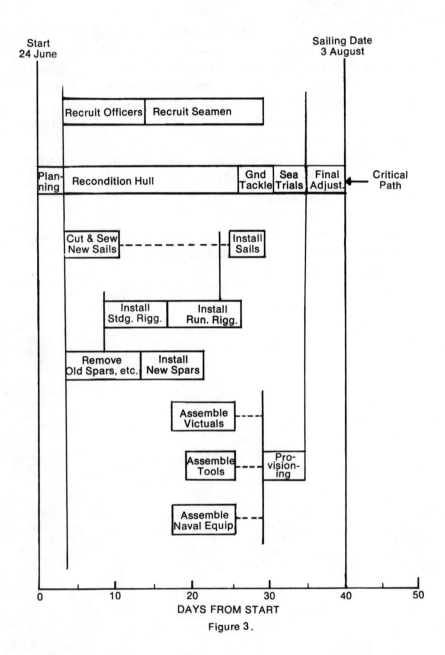

Figure 3.

IV

MEASURING PROGRESS
FOR THE MONEY:
*The Status Index**

In most projects, both defense and nondefense, time and money are reported as if they are independent of each other: progress is ahead or behind schedule, and costs are within or over budget. These meager comparisons, however detailed, are inadequate for project control and visibility.

"Are we getting progress for the money? Where are the trouble spots? What are the trends—are things getting better or worse? How will we come out compared to what we expected?" These are the questions that need answers at each level—task manager, project manager, government programs manager, Secretary of Defense, congressional committee. A control technique that provides the answers is needed. One means of doing this is the Status Index, which measures progress for the money spent.

---

*For a more complete description, see Baumgartner, *Project Management,* pp. 43–60 and 175–177.

CONCEPT

Essentially, the Status Index measures the *expected* cost for an element of work against the *actual* cost of the element. For instance, if a task was estimated to cost $400,000 at completion and winds up costing $500,000, the task manager spent $500,000 doing a job that was "worth" $400,000. He got only 80 percent value for the money spent ($400,000 output in product value, versus 500,000 input in money). This can be expressed as a simple index number, .8, to indicate cost/progress status.

If the task manager expected to spend $400,000 and actually spends $360,000 for the task, the Status Index is 1.1; he has gotten more progress for the money than expected. If he spent $400,000, as expected, his Status Index is 1.0, or par for the course. Where the Status Index is less than 1.0, he's in trouble.

The Status Index can be computed in two ways (by comparing actual versus planned costs upon completing particular milestones, or by a formula using PERT status that gives the same results). These enable the project manager to take corrective action before finding that his tiger has ambushed him. He can get continual readings of "money's worth" because for each element there is a dollar budget that corresponds to milestone progress.

If the project manager were to wait until completion of a particular task, of course, it would be too late to do anything about it if he's in trouble. But he can take a Status Index reading at any time, from beginning to end, and see not only how he stands but also how he's likely to fare in the future. In practice, these readings would normally be at two-week intervals, the typical PERT interval.

APPLICATION

In a project having ten to thirty tasks, each of which may have five to ten subtasks, it is easy to overlook a problem area unless the project manager has a simple, systematic way of spotting trouble. A task that is going well as a whole may mask a subtask that is in trouble, for instance.

The Status Index, as seen in Figure 1, is a way of revealing "money's worth" for each part of a project.

The project manager can see in this case that subtask 4.31 is in trouble (Status Index of .6) whereas, by knowing only the task status as a whole (.9) he might assume (or take the task manager's word) that work within the task is proceeding rather well.

Another use of the Status Index is in forecasting trouble spots, based on trends. Figure 2 is an example.

From the trend of progress for the money in the last three readings, the tiger fighter can see that he's headed for trouble, even though he's hitting 1.0 according to the latest report. With this overview, he would look at reports on tasks and subtasks to isolate the cause of the trend, and would concentrate his attention on these areas.

These two examples show the use of the Status Index in providing in-depth visibility for a particular point in time, and for showing trends over an extended period of time. Other applications of the Status Index are in forecasting costs at completion; stratifying project elements according to "money's worth"; and evaluating the effectiveness of project planning. It is also a way of measuring the effectiveness of managers, within a project or between projects, even though each is developing a unique end-item.

CURRENT PROJECT STATUS

| | Status Indices | | | |
	Project	Task	Subtask	Black Box
Project	1.0			
*	*	*	*	*
Task 3		1.1		
Subtask 3.1			1.1	
3.2			1.0	
3.3			1.1	
3.4			.8	
3.5			.9	
Task 4		.9		
Subtask 4.1			1.0	
4.2			.9	
4.3			.9	
4.31				.6
4.32				1.1
*	*	*	*	*
Task 15		.9		
*	*	*	*	*

Figure 1.

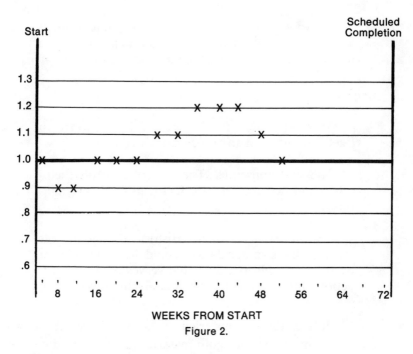

WEEKS FROM START

Figure 2.

COMPARISON WITH OTHER SYSTEMS

To be effective and practical, a cost/schedule system for controlling a project

MUST:

☐ Be "actionable"; that is, serve as a basis for action, rather than merely providing information.

☐ Be applicable at all levels. It must apply from the lowest planned level (such as sub-subtask, or black box) to the highest (total project), and apply for Army, Navy or Air Force programs.

☐ Use existing data: existing planning data and existing cost and progress data.

☐   Give precision, in order to take management
action by exception; i.e., to enable management to
concentrate attention on the out-of-bed situations.

SHOULD:

☐   Serve to forecast. Forewarned is forearmed in
tiger-fighting as in any other kind of combat.

☐   Be cost conscious. The cost of controls themselves can become a major factor in DOD expenditures.

☐   Be simple and concise. Historically, the project
manager has so much data he could drown in it. What
he needs is only the data that serves as a basis for
action, and a simple means of analyzing this data.

Most of the systems tried in the past have been dino-
saurs, huge monsters that gulp massive quantities of data and
belch it out in rearranged form. The basic problem was not so
much their size and complexity, however, but their purpose:
they failed to meet the "musts" of a cost/schedule control
system.

The Status Index is a new way of looking at an old problem. It differs from C/SCSC and PERT/Cost in effectiveness,
simplicity, and in visibility provided. It bears some similarities
to the input-output method used by some contractors, but differs
in other key respects.

CONCLUSION

For individuals concerned with the management of defense projects, project data is useful only as a basis for taking

action to meet cost, schedule, and technical objectives. By the use of a simple technique such as the Status Index, the cost of project controls can be greatly reduced and, more important, the overall cost of programs can be reduced. The impact of reducing project costs by several percentage points, at $200 million per percent, is considerable.

Industry is not likely to use a technique of this type, however, unless DOD points the way.

Notes

CHAPTER 2

[1]David R. Maxey, "The Waste...How to Cut the Budget," *Look,* 26 August 1969, pp. 32–33.

[2]Richard F. Kaufman, "As Eisenhower Was Saying...," *New York Times Magazine,* 22 June 1969, p. 10. Mr. Kaufman is an economist on the staff of the Joint Economic Subcommittee on Economy in Government, headed by Senator Proxmire, and is an associate fellow of the Institute for Policy Studies.

[3]Reprinted with permission from John Stanley Baumgartner, *Project Management* (Homewood, Illinois: Richard D. Irwin, Inc., 1963), p. 157.

[4]George Gallup, "52% Think Too Much Is Spent On Defense," © American Institute of Public Opinion. Reprinted in the *Los Angeles Times,* 14 August 1969.

[5]Joseph Kraft, "Chaining the Defense Monster," *Los Angeles Times,* 26 September 1969.

CHAPTER 3

[1]William McGaffin and Robert Gruenberg, "Military-Industrial Complex Reaches Into All Our Lives," *Chicago Daily News.* Reprinted in the *Los Angeles Times,* 13 April 1969. Reprinted here with permission from the *Chicago Daily News.*

[2]Pages 294, 11, 48, 121, 12, 20. Reprinted by permission of the publisher from *New Products/New Profits,* edited by Elizabeth Marting, © 1964 by the American Management Association, Inc.

[3]*Ibid.,* p. 106.

[4]*Ibid.,* p. 15.

[5] *Ibid.,* p. 278.

[6] Walter J. Talley, Jr., *The Profitable Product* (New Jersey: Prentice-Hall, Inc., 1965), p. 11.

[7] "Defense: Will U.S. Shrink Its Global Role?" *Business Week,* 7 June 1969, p. 144.

CHAPTER 4

[1] Fred J. Cook, *The Warfare State* (New York: The MacMillan Company, 1962), p. 22. He continues with, "This mere fact (*sic*) has led to inevitable suspicions of influence peddling. So far, proof is lacking, though the grounds for suspicion seem more than ample. . . ." Suspicion will serve as proof, however, where The Guilty Bastard has been prejudged.

CHAPTER 5

[1] Sen. George McGovern, "The Looming Spectre of a Permanent Arms Industry," *Business Today,* Summer 1969, p. 35.

[2] *Los Angeles Times,* 3 June 1969.

[3] *Defense Industry Profit Review,* Logistics Management Institute, LMI Task 69-1, March 1969.

[4] *Ibid.,* p. 46.

[5] *Ibid.,* p. 18.

[6] *Ibid.,* p. 17

[7] *Ibid.,* p. 15.

[8] *Ibid.,* p. 46.

[9] Richard F. Kaufman, "As Eisenhower Was Saying . . . ," *New York Times Magazine,* 22 June 1969, p. 69.

[10] *Armed Services Procurement Regulations,* 3-405.6.

[11] ASPR 15-205.17.

[12] ASPR 15-205.1.

[13] ASPR 15-205.11.

[14] ASPR 15-205.8.

[15] ASPR 15-205.2.

[16] ASPR 15-303.4.

[17] LMI Study, op. cit., p. 19.

[18] *Ibid.,* p. 19.

[19] ASPR 8-701, 8-702.

[20] ASPR 8-205.

[21] William D. Phelan, Jr., "The 'Complex' Society Marches On," *Ripon Forum,* January 1969, p. 19.

[22] Allen T. Demaree, "Defense Profits: the Hidden Issues," *Fortune,* 1 August 1969, p. 83.

[23] *Ibid.*

[24] ASPR E-510.1.

[25] "The Pressure Is On Profits," *Business Week*, 2 August 1969, p. 58.

[26] "Profits on Defense Contracts," *Electronic Industries Association*, 14 April 1969.

[27] Michael Getler, "The Complex-Complex," *Aerospace Technology*, 1 January 1968, p. 58.

CHAPTER 6

[1] *The Economics of Military Procurement*, produced by the Joint (Congressional) Economic Committee's Economy in Government Subcommittee, May 1969.

[2] ASPR 4-205.7.

CHAPTER 7

[1] Tristram Coffin, *The Passion of the Hawks: Militarism In Modern America* (New York: Macmillan, 1964), p. 158.

[2] "The Great Manhunt," *Business Week*, 10 August 1957, p. 156—during another era's buffalo hunt.

[3] General Douglas MacArthur, in an address to the National Association of Manufacturers in December, 1954.

CHAPTER 11

[1] Walter J. Talley, Jr., *The Profitable Product* (New Jersey: Prentice-Hall, Inc., 1965), quoting Carl F. Prutton (Director and consultant to FMC Corp.) on the need for urgency, in a 1961 Perkins Medal Address to the American Section of the Society of Chemical Industry.

[2]"Planning for Growth—The Nature and Importance of Product Development," by Dr. Philip Marvin of the American Management Association.

[3]Richard Armstrong, "Military-Industrial Complex—Russian Style," *Fortune*, 1 August 1969, p. 85.

[4]*Los Angeles Times*, 28 August 1969.

CHAPTER 12

[1]"International Outlook," *Business Week*, 3 August 1957, p. 105.

[2]"International Outlook," *Business Week*, 17 August 1957, p. 133.

[3]"International Outlook," *Business Week*, 24 August 1957, p. 127.

[4]"Red Missile Shakes Pentagon," *Business Week* 31 August 1957, p. 30.

[5]"Russia Balks at Arms Control," *Business Week*, 7 September 1957, p. 30.

[6]"Russia Takes Lead in Missiles," *Business Week*, 12 October 1957, p. 39.

[7]"The Trend. How To Regain the Lead in Missiles," *Business Week*, 12 October 1957, p. 204.

[8]"Washington Outlook," *Business Week*, 12 October 1957, p. 55.

[9]"Sputnik Hardens Kremlin's Line," *Business Week*, 19 October 1957, p. 39.

[10]"The Trend. Soviets Put Their Challenge Into Words," *Business Week*, 19 October 1957, p. 204.

[11] "International Outlook," *Business Week,* 19 October 1957, p. 149.

[12] "The Trend. The Nation Waits for Washington," *Business Week,* 26 October 1957, p. 204.

[13] "Washington's First Steps," *Business Week,* 26 October 1957, p. 41.

[14] "International Outlook," *Business Week,* 26 October 1957, p. 147.

[15] "The Battle of Defense Builds Up," *Business Week,* 11 January 1958, p. 25.

CHAPTER 13

[1] From the copyrighted article " 'Witch Hunt' Against Military? A Warning," *U.S. News and World Report,"* 23 July 1969, p. 16.

[2] "Our Security Lies Beyond Weapons," *Look,* 26 August 1969, p. 37.

[3] J.-J. Servan-Schreiber, *The American Challenge* (New York: Atheneum House, Inc., 1968), pp. 27–28.

[4] *Ibid.,* pp. 63–67.

[5] Elmer B. Staats, Comptroller General, before the Proxmire Committee, 11 November 1968.

[6] "I'm Not Involved Anymore," by William F. Russell, *Sports Illustrated,* August 4, 1969, p. 18.

[7] Sen. George McGovern, *Business Today,* Summer 1969, p. 38.

Suggested Readings

BOOKS

Baker, Bruce N. and Eris, Rene L. *An Introduction to PERT-CPM*. Homewood, Ill.: Richard D. Irwin, Inc., 1964.

Baumgartner, John Stanley. *Project Management*. Homewood, Ill.: Richard D. Irwin, Inc., 1963.

Coffin, Tristram. *The Passion of the Hawks: Militarism in Modern America*. New York: Macmillan, 1964.

Contract Clauses, Armed Services Procurement Regulation. Chicago, Ill.: Commerce Clearing House, 1970.

Cook, Fred J. *The Warfare State*. New York: The MacMillan Company, 1962.

Duscha, Julius. *Arms, Money and Politics*. New York: Ives Washburn, 1965.

Enke, Stephen. *Defense Management*. Englewood Cliffs, N.J.: Prentice-Hall, 1967.

Galbraith, John K. *How to Control the Military*. New York: Signet Books, New American Library, Inc., 1969.

Jackson, Henry M., Senator, ed. *The National Security Council*. New York, Washington, London: Praeger, 1965.

Lapp, Ralph E. *The Weapons Culture*. New York: W. W. Norton & Co., Inc., 1968.

Marting, Elizabeth, ed. *New Products/New Profits*. New York: American Management Association, 1964.

McNamara, Robert S. *The Essence of Security*. New York: Harper, 1968.

Peck, Merton J. and Scherer, Frederic M.: *The Weapons Acquisition Process*. Harvard University: Division of Research, Graduate School of Business Administration, 1962.

Scherer, Frederic M. *The Weapons Acquisition Process: Economic Incentives*. Harvard University: Division of Research, Graduate School of Business Administration, 1962.

Servan-Schreiber, J.-J. *The American Challenge*. New York: Atheneum, 1968.

Talley, Walter J., Jr. *The Profitable Product*. Englewood Cliffs, N.J.: Prentice-Hall, 1965.

Thayer, George. *The War Business*. New York: Simon and Schuster, Inc., 1969.

Weidenbaum, Murray L. *Arms and the American Economy*. Washington University: Department of Economics, 1967.

PERIODICALS

Among the many articles on the military-industrial complex are these feature articles:

"The Military-Industrial Complex," *Newsweek*, 9 June 1969, pp. 74–87.

"Military-Industrial Complex; The Facts vs. the Fictions," *U.S. News and World Report*, 21 April 1969, pp. 60–63.

"The Military: Servant or Master of Policy?" *Time*, 11 April 1969, pp. 20–26.

Glossary of
Abbreviations

MIC   military-industrial complex

MIPLUC   military-industrial-political-labor-university
           complex

LEEPSMIC   labor-economic-educational-political-scientific-
           military-industrial complex

R&D   research and development

DSRV   deep submersible rescue vehicle

DOD   Department of Defense

RDTE   research, development, test and evaluation

T/O&E   tactical units' tables of organization and
           equipment

RFP   request for proposal

PM   project manager

LMI   Logistics Management Institute

CPPC   cost plus percentage of cost

ASPR   Armed Services Procurement Regulations

IFB   invitation for bid

D&F	determination and findings
CPFF	cost plus fixed fee
FFP	firm fixed-price
FPI	fixed-price incentive
CPIF	cost plus incentive fee
ASBCA	Armed Services Board of Contract Appeals
G&A	general and administrative
QA	quality assurance
GAO	General Accounting Office
CO	Contracting Officer
WBS	work breakdown structure
PERT	program evaluation and review technique
CPM	critical path method
JPL	Jet Propulsion Laboratories
VE	value engineering
AOA	American Ordnance Association

P/C   PERT/Cost

C/SCSC   cost/schedule control system criteria

MBT   main battle tank

DEW   distant early warning line

LZ   landing zone

ICBM   intercontinental ballistics missile

FOBS   fractional orbit bombardment system

AMC   Army Materiel Command

This book was designed by Kay McRee and typeset by Continental Graphics, a Division of Republic Corporation, Los Angeles, California, in 11 point Times Roman with 3 point leading. The display type used for the Chapter Openings and Contents is Aurora Condensed. The text and jacket were printed by offset lithography by Publishers Press, Salt Lake City, Utah. The text paper is 60# Antique and the jacket paper is 80# Roughback Enamel, supplied by Publishers Press. The book was bound in Holliston Mills Natural Finish Payko Cloth by Mountain States Bindery, Salt Lake City, Utah.